# Links

**How to Order:**

Quantity discounts are available from the publisher, Prima Publishing, P.O. Box 1260LR, Rocklin, CA 95677; telephone (916) 624-5718. On your letterhead include information concerning the intended use of the books and the number of books you wish to purchase.

*U.S. Bookstores and Libraries:* Please submit all orders to St. Martin's Press, 175 Fifth Avenue, NY, NY 10010; telephone (212) 674-5151.

# Links

## An Exploration Into the Mind, Heart, and Soul of Golf

**Prima Publishing**
P.O. Box 1260LR
Rocklin, CA 95677
(916) 624-5718

Jacket design by The Dunlavey Studio
Typesetting by Jay Tee Graphics Ltd.

Prima Publishing
Rocklin, CA

Published in the United States by Prima Publishing through special arrangement with Random House of Canada Limited

**Library of Congress Cataloging-in-Publication Data**

Rubenstein, Lorne.
　　Links: an exploration into the mind, heart, and soul of golf / by Lorne Rubenstein.
　　　　p.　　cm.
　　Reprint. Originally published: Toronto · Random House of Canada. 1990.
　　ISBN 1-55958-072-0
　　1. Golf.　I. Title.
GV965.R78　1991
796.352—dc20　　　　　　　　　　　　　　　　　　　　91-7652
　　　　　　　　　　　　　　　　　　　　　　　　　　　CIP

91 92 93 94 RRD 10 9 8 7 6 5 4 3 2 1

*In memory of my father*

# Contents

Preface                                                                    ix

Chapter One: The Soul of the Game                                           1
Chapter Two: To Have and Have Not:
        In Search of the Swing                                17
Chapter Three: Mind Games                                                  37
Chapter Four: In the Zone                                                  57
Chapter Five: Caddying: Along for the Ride                                 73
Chapter Six: Around the World in Eighteen Holes                           95
Chapter Seven: Moe Norman: Golf's Eccentric Genius                       121
Chapter Eight: Speaking of Golf:
        The Language of the Game                             139
Chapter Nine: Links Between Friends                                       157

# Acknowledgments

Many people have encouraged me along the way to this book. I would like to thank Cec Jennings in particular. He was sports editor at *The Globe and Mail* in 1980 when I approached him with the idea of a weekly golf column. He saw the merit of such a column and told me to write what I saw and felt about the game. I don't think I would be writing here today if Cec hadn't been sitting at the sports editor's desk at *The Globe* a decade ago.

I enjoyed the work of other golf writers long before I turned to the profession myself. I am grateful for the work and leadership of those who came before me and who are no longer with us: Bernard Darwin, Henry Longhurst, and Pat Ward-Thomas, golf writing's great triumvirate. I also record my appreciation to those writers who continue to grace the pages of the world's newspapers and magazines. Many are my friends; they know who they are, and their work continues to inspire me. I look forward to reading them for many years and to meeting them often on the world's courses.

I also thank the following professional golfers for giving freely of their time to me over the years: Seve Ballesteros, Ben Crenshaw, the late Jack Grout, the late George Knudson, Johnny Miller, Jim Nelford, Jack Nicklaus, Greg Norman, Moe Norman, Curtis Strange, and Tom Watson. Their contributions are apparent in this book.

Other people have helped more directly as this book took shape. The following individuals commented on the manuscript at various stages: James Fitchette, Howard Ganz, Fay Ganz, Jerome Lyons, Bradley Klein, Norman Mogil, and Nell Waldman. I thank them for their suggestions.

My relationship with Random House of Canada has been enjoyable from the moment I met Ed Carson, the publisher, and Doug Pepper, my editor. I thank them for believing in the book, and am especially grateful to Doug for his guidance.

The book would not have developed without the support I received from the staff at the Lucinda Vardey Agency in Toronto. I worked closely with Lucinda Vardey and Linda Turchin. They are caring people in a caring agency.

# Preface

Years ago, while studying in university, I read a paper called "Some Unintended Consequences of Rigorous Research" by psychologist Chris Argyris. Leaving aside the contents of the paper, I am reminded by the title that unpredictable things can happen when one sets out on a certain path. The path I've taken has been as a golfer and golf writer, and the consequences of doing so have often been surprising and always pleasant. My research has been conducted in warm, sunny places around the world wherever people whack a little ball around a course for pleasure or profit, and sometimes both. It has been a most congenial way of earning a living.

As a boy, I played many sports. But golf was special. Most summers I accompanied my father to golf tournaments. One day my father took me to watch as Arnold Palmer and Gary Player played an exhibition at a Toronto club. Like any enthusiastic youngster, I waited for their autographs. Then there was the time my dad took me to a tournament at the Oakland Hills Country Club outside Detroit, where I followed a threesome that included Palmer and Ben Hogan. The third member of the group hit his long approach shot to a par-four within fifteen feet of the hole; Palmer put his within eight feet; Hogan watched these two fine shots, stared down the flagstick, then rifled his shot less than three feet from the hole. I was mesmerized. My dad, who knew something about sports — he'd played some pro football in western Canada — had opened a new world to me: a world where a person could be alone or in company, a world where he could engage himself in a contest with himself, the course, or his opponent. My father died just as I started writing this book in May 1989, but his presence was strong throughout my work on it. We got to know each other as we walked together at golf tournaments, as we played rounds together. It's one of those unintended consequences of the game: You go out to make pars, and you make friends.

I practiced as a kid, and before long I was entering junior tournaments. However, I didn't have much success, being too introspective for the game. It always bothered me when I hit a bad shot and I wasn't able to walk away without asking why. There was a discrepancy between practice and the real thing. I turned to golf magazines for the answer, wondering how I could hit the ball beautifully in practice but falter in tournaments. I'm still asking those questions and learning that even Jack Nicklaus, Seve Ballesteros, and Greg Norman are doing the same. I'm intrigued by this aspect of golf; every player, no matter his or her abilities, agonizes over the game. That means nearly every golfer becomes thoughtful about the game, which makes for fine conversation.

My interest in golf led me in the summer of 1970 to the London Hunt course, 120 miles west of Toronto, my birthplace. The Canadian Open was being played there. I signed on to caddie for Bob Murphy, then one of the better U.S. PGA Tour players. But as it turned out he had brought his own caddie. Luckily for me, I ran into Bob Dickson and worked for him instead. This was an unintended consequence; Dickson had won both the United States and British Amateurs and was regarded as a top prospect in professional golf. We became friends, and I caddied for him during the next seven or eight summers, at perhaps two or three tournaments a season. Inside the world of golf, I began to meet some of the pros. Dickson was very good about introducing me to them. Invariably, I found them willing to talk about themselves and the game.

I really didn't begin to write about golf, though, until later. In the summer of 1974 I played a club championship at the old Uplands course in north Toronto. I had led for three rounds after shooting seventy-one, seventy-seven, seventy, but I seemed to take on a different personality in the last round. My smooth swing became forced; I walked fast. In short, I choked, and when I came home I poured it all out in my journal. I never thought it would be published.

It wasn't. An editor for one of the top U.S. golf magazines read the piece and told me he would pay me $400 for it. However, a year and many phone calls and letters later, it still wasn't published. In fact, nobody at the magazine had heard of it. The editor had apparently fled the magazine, not to mention his family. Still, I got the message that people actually made a living writing about golf. Another unintended consequence.

Further such experiences followed. I was playing golf at Uplands one summer day when I ran into a student from the University of Guelph, fifty miles west of Toronto. He told me that he had worked with Dr. Richard Lonetto in the psychology department and that we had some interests in common. Before long I'd enrolled in the M.A. program there under Lonetto's direction. Lonetto was a sports enthusiast whose game on the streets of Brooklyn had been stick-ball, not golf. But he became interested in golf after we met at the university and eventually worked and continues to work with some athletes on psychological techniques to improve their play. We've kept each other thinking, and some of our best discussions have been while we were golfing. Meeting Lonetto was yet another unintended and happy consequence.

By 1975 I'd acquired my M.A. and had started work on a doctorate. I considered studying the psychology of golf, but decided I was analytical enough about the game. Meanwhile, I noticed a poster at Uplands saying that the Royal Canadian Golf Association was moving from downtown Toronto to the Glen Abbey Golf Club, where it was going to start a golf museum. I figured the RCGA might need a curator and applied for a job that didn't exist with qualifications I didn't have. I was in my late twenties and knew as much about museum work as I did about flying a plane — nothing. But I got the part-time job, which meant I spent a day or two a week cataloging hickory golf clubs, dusty, dirty trophies, faded photographs, and old books. I also joined the Golf Collectors' Society around the same time. At the time, its members numbered about fifty and collected anything and everything about golf from rare clubs to books to decorative items. Its membership has since increased to around 2,000. At the university, meanwhile, I read Herbert Warren Wind's articles on the Masters in the *New Yorker* when I should have been reading for my doctorate and followed up with Bernard Darwin in old *Country Life* magazines. And I started writing for Canadian Open programs, thinking that one day I might write more about golf.

Further unintended consequences followed. I went to England to play in the 1977 British Amateur at Ganton, the home course of Harry Vardon, winner of the British Open championship six times between 1896 and 1914. There I met and had a practice round with

Jim Nelford, a British Columbia golfer who had won the 1975 and 1976 Canadian Amateurs. We stayed in touch after the tournament, and after he turned pro in 1977 I caddied for him from time to time. That led directly to my writing a weekly golf column for *The Globe and Mail,* Canada's national newspaper. I've been writing the column since 1980.

One thing led to another. I had written a piece for *Toronto Life* to coincide with the 1979 Canadian Open. While I worked on it, editor Don Obe gave me the best piece of advice I've had. "Just write what you know and feel about the game," he told me after I had turned in my first draft.

I never finished the doctorate in psychology, choosing instead to follow golf. Wherever I traveled, there were new people to meet, people who were captivated by golf. The brilliant Canadian golfer George Knudson and I became close friends, and in the summer of 1987, shortly after he had been diagnosed as having lung cancer, we did a book together. Knudson died in January 1989; he was a warm-hearted man who wanted only that people enjoy golf to the fullest. He certainly helped me get more out of the game.

One of the most enjoyable aspects of my work is the travel. Golf is an international game, and I've covered it in Scotland, Ireland, England, Italy, Portugal, Africa, Japan, and Indonesia. I've been to British Opens, U.S. Opens, the Masters, PGA Championships, the World Cup, and the Ryder Cup. I've learned that golfers the world over are very much the same. They all imagine that the latest innovation in clubhead materials may help, and it sometimes does, just often enough to fuel their dreams. They read the latest swing theories, believing they might find the answer. Sometimes they improve, for a short time anyway. And they all remember the day they played so well. The result is that when they meet at golf courses all over the world, they always have something to talk about. Usually they can't stop talking about it.

I've met many golfers, along with the people who teach them. Dare I say it, but I believe my golf might be getting better because of these encounters. The improvement is another unintended consequence. Or maybe it's that I'm more relaxed about golf. I don't know. But I do see every round as a gift these days. It's just nice to be out on the course.

Yet I also yearn to return to competition. After all, I've played some good golf and have even won a few tournaments: the Eastern Ontario Amateur in 1972, when I shot seventy-four, sixty-nine in the thirty-six-hole competition; the Golf Writers Association of America Championship in 1984 — my first "major" — when I shot seventy-six at the Dunes Club in Myrtle Beach in cold wind; my colleagues said it wasn't surprising that I had won under such conditions — after all, as a Canadian, I should have done well in weather more suited to ice hockey. Then there was the time I shot seventy-five at the Olympic Club in San Francisco the day after the 1987 U.S. Open, playing the same tees and pins the pros had during the final round. These rounds suggest to me that I can play the game.

But such rounds are infrequent. More often I can't settle into the shot comfortably. I feel that my head is buried between my shoulders, or that my hands don't fit the club. Or I become too aware of a specific swing position. My mind jangles with any number of thoughts about swing positions, most of which I've tried, incantations to lift me out of my golfing fog. Playing by feel alone, I feel too much. Playing by rote and mechanics, I think too much.

Which golfer is the real me? The seventy-five-shooter at Olympic, or the troubled golfer I have too often turned into? Like many golfers, I seek consistency, but find only wild oscillations of performance. I'm the golfer you meet on the course every day, everywhere. I take the game seriously, even though I don't play it for my livelihood. I'd like to find the golfer who doesn't take it seriously, who doesn't want to improve, who can abide a bad shot. There are, of course, plenty of bad shots to abide. Golfers who enjoy the game to the fullest are able to put the bad shot aside, at least long enough to hit the next shot. There's always another shot. It's surprising how badly we feel about a shot that we've just hit, but how quickly we can forget it. Golf lets us figure things out. It gives us time to make the right choices.

Four hours on the course are four hours of contemplation. We stand over a shot and remember the beauty we hit there six years ago, or, equally likely, the terrible shot we hit last week. Whatever our state of mind, we feel away from things, outside real life. We are in a private world where, as golfing legend Bobby Jones suggested, things are so concentrated that we can't think about our off-course worlds. Golf becomes fact, life off the course becomes fiction. We are in a mostly natural environment — at least it's all grass — while the surface of the outside world is increasingly artificial. We are restored on the course. We can come to ourselves.

But golf is not a factual representation of the world, notwithstanding the grass, the blueberries in the woods, the wind at our backs. It is not a metaphor for life. The golfer who plays poorly under pressure may yet make the right business decision. The golfer who rants and raves when he misses a shot may be calm off the course.

Golf encourages a dream state. It allows our minds and imaginations to roam. I can play a hole and think of how Tom Watson would have handled it. I can compose an outline for an article as I walk between shots, or read a page or two in a book while waiting on the tee. I can notice a golfer three holes over in the forest and wonder how he's ever going to get out of there. Or I can simply daydream while playing. Golf encourages reverie. To be part of golf is to come upon stories, to become a story, to tell stories.

# ONE

# The Soul of the Game

The Royal Worlington and Newmarket Golf Club in England is the finest nine-hole course in the world. It is ten miles from Cambridge University and lies hidden near the village of Mildenhall — "Take your first turn at the pub, and then you'll come across Golf Links Road," a woman in the local postal office had told me. Royal Worlington is basic golf. The land is the same as it was a century ago prior to the nine holes being laid out: not an artificial lake dug, fairways and greens not watered but for what falls from the sky, the landscape featureless, or seemingly so, except for the tees and greens and wild-looking bunkers and rough. Twosomes only are allowed, which makes for fast play — less than two and a half hours for two trips around the nine holes — and the game most often played is match play, where golfers play hole for hole against one another. The golfer who wins two and one is two holes up on his opponent with just one hole to play. Game over, in other words. No need to play the last.

For me, though, the game was just beginning. It was early November 1988, and I was traveling up from Cambridge to play Royal Worlington. I was looking for the dimensions of the game as they might be encompassed in one century-old course. My plan was to immerse myself in the course, feel its charms, and, I hoped, discover why my English golfing pals had suggested I put Worlington on my must-play list, and then return and write this book. What made the game special to its millions of participants around the world? How did the ingredients that seemed so out of keeping with modern golf generate what my friends had called "atmosphere"? I would soon find out.

Driving to Royal Worlington, I wondered which golf professional I would choose to play the course with, if I could. My mind settled quickly on Ben Crenshaw. Crenshaw is an accomplished golf historian who appreciates and feels the game deeply. He has a comprehensive library of the game in his home in Austin, Texas, and has also written well on his own. He belongs to the Golf Collectors' Society, of which I am also a member. I share his passion for first-class golf writing.

I had visited Crenshaw in late 1981 for a story I was writing, and in the years since we had spoken often of the pleasures of golf. As he had written in a letter, "Golf is at its best when you are closest to nature in a serene setting with holes before you that stimulate thought and intrigue the mind." Royal Worlington was reputed to do just that. Now, nearly thirty years after I first put my hand on a golf club, I wanted to address certain questions directly. I'd formed many impressions while playing and writing golf, but I felt that Royal Worlington was the place to begin to consider them seriously. It was supposed to be a basic course that was as subtle as it was charming. What was the mystery of golf? Why is it such a popular sport? Why had I rarely heard of anybody quitting the game? I felt certain that if I could understand Royal Worlington, I would come closer to understanding the game's appeals. I felt certain that its nine holes would reveal what writers had long referred to as the "soul" of golf. I wouldn't be playing with Crenshaw, but it would be easy enough to imagine him there. In some ways he belonged there, since he had such a feel for the history of the game. His enthusiasm had arisen full-blown when he competed as a teen-ager in the United States Junior at The Country Club in Brookline, Massachusetts. Each competitor was given a copy of Francis Ouimet's book, *A Game of Golf: A Book of Reminiscences*, written in 1932. Ouimet had won the 1913 United States Open at The Country Club, defeating Englishmen Harry Vardon and Ted Ray in an eighteen-hole play-off. The win signaled the rise of American golf and led to an upsurge of interest in the game in the United States. It also sparked Crenshaw's lifelong fascination with golf. "I remember looking at this book," Crenshaw had told me at his home in Austin, "and thinking, 'I'm playing here. I'm playing on this course where this great event happened.' "

I reasoned that playing Royal Worlington might well arouse similar feelings in me. The club has long been home to golfers from nearby Cambridge University, and a list of the university's golf club captains includes Harry Colt, a former law student at the school who designed Formby and Royal Liverpool, or Hoylake, as it's known in England. I'd played these courses and had also been over the Toronto Golf Club, another Colt gem. Then there was Bernard Darwin, the doyen of British golf writers who wrote his first article for *The Times* of London in 1907 and continued as golf correspondent for forty-six years. Royal Worlington and Newmarket seemed the right place for me. Visiting the club and playing its course would give me the opportunity to further understand and appreciate the game's authenticity. I had been thinking about what had attracted me many years before to the game. Maybe Worlington would connect me to my own golfing past.

Toronto, 1962. First, for me, came a long, wide valley flanked by hills on either side. Once farmland and now destined for highway, it was an open stretch of land where, as a teen-ager, I could hit golf balls. I often wandered over the hills and rough ground that made up my course. The Ontario Ministry of Transport would soon pave these lands as it widened what was then called Highway 401. The new road would force me to take my clubs elsewhere, but for now there was golf, shots to be hit. Augusta National it wasn't, but who cared?

Clumps of weedy turf were my fairways. Much of the ground was cracked, fissures created by the dry, cool spring winds. Still, there was turf enough for golf, and where there wasn't, I'd improvise. I liked golf because I could hit a ball, or an object, wherever I walked, on or off my course. Trees are targets. Stones on the ground are balls. Branches work as clubs. Can I hit the ball from here to there? How many strokes will it take? What did I do right on that particular shot? And what went wrong then? Why didn't the ball fly properly?

My highway course was ideal. It was open, which provided freedom. It allowed inventiveness, so that I could create golf holes. It was spacious, which meant I could roam at will. And it was secluded. It offered what I have come to think is one of golf's major appeals, captured in the title of a book that Gretel Ehrlich wrote about ranching in Wyoming. *The Solace of Open Spaces* has nothing to do with golf, but the idea expressed in the title is vital to the game. Call my retreat Highway Hideaway Golf Course. I've looked for it since and have found it wherever golfers gather.

Settled in, I found a piece of hard ground upon which I placed my ball. The parched ground ran forever, or at least as far as I might hit a drive when I really caught one. I traveled lightly: driver and three-wood, three-, five-, seven- and nine-irons, two-way putter, all bunched into a plaid, stovepipe golf bag. I carried fifteen or twenty golf balls. My favorite ball was the Ontario Pro; alas, it was soft. Never mind, though. I wasn't yet at the stage where I thought I needed Titleists. I was a kid hitting golf balls into the setting sun. I'd found my game.

And what a game. I could play alone, which suited my solitary nature. My mistakes were my own, as were my triumphs. But I'm sure I didn't think of these aspects then; I enjoyed hitting the ball, setting up to the shot, taking the club back and turning away from the target, twisting back, then returning. Such sweet, clean contact when everything happened in sync. I enjoyed watching the flight of the ball, higher and farther than a baseball, with more curve than a football, taking so much longer to arrive at its destination than a hockey puck. And even when it arrived it hadn't yet reached its final resting place; the ball bounced, caromed, ricocheted. Highway

Hideaway Golf Course was not a true course, but in its essentials it offered all a person really needed for one: room to move; a starting place; a target — a discarded Coke bottle I'd placed 343 measured steps away, just over a hump in the ground. I could pretend I was Arnold Palmer with a shot to win the United States Open. This was simple, unadorned golf in which I could set my will free in a childlike way. Imagination was everything as I made up my course and invented shots. The idea was to hit the ball and hit it again until I got it in the hole, or in this case, until it rattled off the pop bottle. That was golf. It's still golf.

April 1984. It's the last day of the Masters, and Ben Crenshaw is on the tenth green that sits at the bottom of a hill in a woodland of pine trees. He faces a putt of a full sixty feet, across the back third of the green, up and over contours that only a golfer with experience on Augusta National's undulating greens can read, that only a gifted putting stroke can handle. At ten-under par for the tournament, Crenshaw is in the thick of contention. He has yet to win a major championship, and there isn't a tournament he'd like to win more than the Masters. It's played at the Augusta National Golf Club, the cathedral in the pines, as it's often referred to, and Crenshaw's idol Bobby Jones was the inspiration behind the course and tournament. When Crenshaw has gone through tough times, he's often turned to Jones's writings for solace. "I didn't do anything for five days," he said during one bad spell of ball-striking, "except think and read books. I guess I have every book written by or about Bobby Jones. I always go back to some of his books because he wrote with such great style, so lucid, and he had a very natural way of reflecting about the game."

From 1923 to 1929, Jones won two British Opens, four United States Amateurs, and three United States Opens. In 1930 he won the British and United States Opens and Amateurs and then retired, though he was only twenty-eight. He then went to work on the Augusta National Golf Club along with New York investment banker Clifford Roberts and Scottish course designer Alister MacKenzie. The property had been a nursery and was a dreamscape of flowering bushes, a rolling magnificence that Jones felt was meant for a golf course and that would make a visitor sigh with his first view of it. The course did just that after it opened in 1933, and Jones invited his golfing friends the following year to participate in what was first known as the Augusta National Invitation tournament. Jones finally agreed to call it the Masters in 1938; it's been that since, an annual rite of spring that all golfers look forward to, and none more so than Crenshaw.

Crenshaw speaks of Jones with the utmost respect. "He is an idol of mine, even though he is long gone," he told Texas writer and friend Mickey Herskowitz. "He had a freewheeling sort of swing, and if people wanted to criticise something in my swing, I guess they could say his swing was sort of wild, too."

Back at that 1984 Masters, Crenshaw surveyed his long putt on the tenth green in the final round. Crenshaw is a master putter. His long backswing flows into a gently accelerating throughstroke. He catches the ball at just the right point, and then it comes off the putterface like a parent's hand caressing a child's back. So loose, so gentle, so effective.

Crenshaw was one shot ahead of Tom Kite. His caddie, Carl Jackson, helped him read the putt, and then Crenshaw stroked the ball. It rolled and rolled and rolled, and when it fell into the hole with perfect speed it seemed reasonable to assume that this Masters belonged to Crenshaw. Playing freely, he went on to defeat Tom Watson by two shots. The victory was sweet. Crenshaw had won the Masters by being himself. I watched him and I saw that golf allows us access to the uninhibited self. Golf can set it free, as it did for Crenshaw that spring afternoon at Augusta National.

November 1988. The mellow English countryside northeast of London rolls by as I make my way toward Royal Worlington and Newmarket. I've been writing about golf for a decade or so and have visited and played many courses. A map of my world — mental and actual — would connect courses much as a musician's might connect concert halls he's played, performances he's given. The Highway Hideaway course is long gone but I still know it as my golfing birthplace. There was also my back yard on Joicey Boulevard, the street where I grew up in Toronto. I enjoyed chipping golf balls around the yard to holes I had dug in the ground. And there was scratchy Tuxedo Golf Course in Winnipeg — my dad's birthplace — where he, a self-described "screwed-up left-hander" as a golfer, first showed me that it was possible to enjoy the game even when things weren't going well. I also realized that things would soon improve; golf was like that, for a decent swing always showed up. I can't forget the beauty of Banff and Jasper, Alberta, where a golf ball hangs high against the mountains, reaches its apex, and then falls out of the sky like a bird landing on the branch of a tree. There was the Anegasaki course in Japan, where I had a round with Keiichi Harada, a professor of American literature at Chiba University who translates P.G. Wodehouse's golf stories into Japanese. "I've done the first nine stories," he told me one December afternoon as he huddled over a short putt, "and I hope I can convince the publisher to do the back nine."

So many courses, so many people, so many new friends, all of us linked by the pleasures we take at the game English writer Henry Longhurst called the Esperanto of sport, a universal language. I have been fortunate to meet the world's golfers — amateur and professional, the dubs and the champions — in the agreeable environments of golf courses.

But what is it about golf that connects us? I enjoy hockey and have often talked about the game with friends. I still play regularly with the same fellows I've skated with since we were teen-agers. But long ago we had moved our two-hour Sunday night game from the freezing outdoor rink to a one-hour session in a heated ice palace in a Toronto suburb. A concession to age? Yes, that, but there is more. We never talk about hockey with the same passion as do golfers about their game. I have a decent slap shot, but I don't discuss technique with my friends: how far to take the stick back, where my elbows should be at the top of the backswing. I have never taken a skating lesson; neither have my friends. Nor do we seek the pure places to play hockey, the back-yard rinks of our youth, the frozen rivers and natural ice. We have withdrawn from elemental hockey, bought fancy equipment, high-tech skates made of titanium and other alloys — the names of which I don't care or need to learn. We're into mastery through technology. We don't think about the mysteries of hockey.

Golf is different. Arnold Haultain wrote a classic book in 1908 called *The Mystery of Golf*. Haultain, who was born in India in 1857 but who later moved to Toronto, also wrote a book called *Hints for Lovers*, and another called *Two Country Walks in Canada*. It's interesting that Haultain chose to write about such apparently diverse subjects. But he was a romantic. He tried to understand things, to put them together. Like him, golfers consumed with the game believe it has links with so many areas. Nobel prize winner Sir Charles Sherrington, the leading physiologist and scholar of the nervous system during the late nineteenth and early twentieth centuries, was so taken by golf that he wrote the foreword to the 1923 book *The Brain and Golf: Some Hints for Golfers from Modern Mental Science*, by C.W. Bailey. Sherrington, a professor of physiology at Oxford, wrote that "the 'ancient game of golf' has a literature of its own; but to relate the *raison d'être* of practical maxims for obtaining proficiency with the clubs to underlying principles of physiology and psychology is a venture at once bold and desirable."

We fail much more frequently in golf than we succeed. Why do we return? It must be more than the successes, rare as they are. It must be the nature of the game, something it does to us, something it brings out of us, the ways in which it engages us on so many levels. It brings us consolation as we walk its open spaces and offers us a subtle balance of companionship and solitude. I walk with a friend down the fairway and we chat. Then we separate to play our respective shots. We meet again at the green. Is this an analogue of the rhythms of meetings and departures that we need, but that we so rarely enjoy in our daily, mostly jangled lives? What does golf touch in us?

I have searched for answers to these questions for the thirty or so years that I have played golf. But not consciously so. I don't care to understand once and for all the game's appeal, only to explore the game, to delve into it. To do that I always return to the courses of the world, there to walk, hear, and feel the game.

I relax on the course and come to myself, and I believe this happens to all golfers now and has happened for the five hundred years that we know golf has been played.

Royal Worlington and Newmarket was founded in 1890. It has served since as the home course for Cambridge University golfers, though it's ten miles away. I've been graced with a warm autumn day as I make my journey through Newmarket's racing country, past the horse farms and the well-known track itself, then right at the Chequers pub at Mildenhall to Golf Links Road. A left turn, a few hundred yards, and I'm at the course.

My first impression of Worlington might have been "So what?" except that many of the best courses hide both their treachery and their pleasures. The lure of golf courses is related to their accumulated lore and history. The game is always more than one sees. Worlington exemplifies this. It's open field, that's all, flat and rectangular. The course is on the left side of the road, except for the final green, and the plain clubhouse is to the right. But I know that I'll find riches there. Having parked my car in the gravelly parking lot, I walk into the clubhouse. There I'm greeted by the club steward, who asks if I'd like to order lunch now since I'll be coming in around noon after my round. He shows me the menu and I place my order. "Vegetable soup and a couple of cheese and chutney sandwiches will be fine," I tell him, and then head out for my solo round. Two golfers are ahead of me, but they'll move quickly.

The first hole at Worlington is a par-five of 486 yards, out-of-bounds fence to the right, and a long, narrow bunker on the left side of the fairway. The theme is immediately established: Play safely and you will have to contend with bunkers, but at least you'll be in play. Take the riskier route — down the right side — and if you bring the shot off you might get home in two. But miss the shot just a smidgen and you could be out of bounds.

Crenshaw would love it here. He hasn't played Royal Worlington, but it's his type of course. I'll need to think. Too many of our modern courses force you to hit just one shot. There are no alternative routes. If there's water, you have to hit over it. The recipe for a difficult course is simple: Just add water. Water hazards when used in moderation add substance to a course; the golfer is required to gauge how far he can carry the ball, and then go ahead and do so. North American courses are full of such shots, too many, I think.

Worlington's bunkers are just the antidote to water. They imply ways of playing the shot while also presenting alternatives. That bunker to the left on the first hole isn't necessarily in play for me, but it keeps me from trying to smash the ball down the left side. It makes a straightforward hole interesting. The wind isn't blowing too hard now, but when it does the shot from this tee becomes downright dangerous. Playing it in a strong right-to-left wind would be quite a challenge. The proper shot would be a fade held against the wind. Left to right when the wind is right to left: That would be the way to control the flight of the ball under such conditions. Wind makes a seemingly open course like Worlington much tighter. Maybe that's why Crenshaw likes the golf in Great Britain; it offers freedom in one sense — those open spaces — but that freedom is also a problem. Fairways become narrow when the wind blows in open spaces.

My drive on the first hole is a good one, some 245 yards out, and in the fairway. I may be able to reach the green with my second shot — it's open in front — but I'd have to hit my best three-wood. I'd like to give it a try, but it's too early in the round for heroics. I want to get into the round slowly, let momentum build. There's no need to go after everything, not yet anyway.

Having decided to lay up short of the green, I choose a two-iron. Weight back, weight through, and on to a balanced finish. But the ball curves slightly further right than I'd like. Taken there by one of the capricious winds that can pick up at any moment at Worlington, it comes to rest forty yards short of the green and off to the right side of the fairway. Now I face an awkward approach to the hole, which is cut in the right corner of the green.

Was it the wind, though, that affected the flight of the ball, or was it the long backswing that I've been working on? I'm 6′3″, which means I can generate good power if I make a full arc as I swing. Crenshaw isn't as tall, but his backswing is long. I decide to stick with the long backswing, which I'm trying to achieve by extending back from the ball. The idea seems right because it means I'll use all of myself. That's natural; why should I restrict my swing?

The theme of restriction is central to golf, and not only with regards to the swing. Having played my way down Worlington's first hole, I understand that it's so pleasant precisely because I had choices. I was allowed to be open-minded, to think. Crenshaw has often said that modern courses restrict us — they close our minds — because they don't present alternatives. Courses such as the Tournament Players' Club in Ponte Vedra, Florida, with its famous island seventeenth green, are examples of penal architecture. There's no choice. The only shot on the par-three is a short iron in the air. It's hit the green or the surrounding lake. There's an undeniable thrill in hitting the green with your first ball. You've done it; you've hit the island seventeenth. It's instant gratification, which is often the primary source of satisfaction in modern course design. It's the kind of shot you discuss with your friends after the round and for long after. Like a hole in one, it can happen to anybody, since anybody can hit one successful shot at the right moment.

But I prefer a more durable satisfaction, as does Crenshaw. He's an advocate of strategic architecture, where the golfer can select from possible routes according to his ability, confidence, and courage. The more risk a golfer takes, the greater the reward when he succeeds. But he doesn't have to choose the more difficult route or go against his will. There are alternatives. Bobby Jones and Alister MacKenzie created a masterpiece of strategic architecture in Augusta National.

Playing well at Augusta National or the Old Course in St. Andrews, Scotland, leaves one with an enduring satisfaction as opposed to the instant gratification that modern, penal courses offer. I won't feel so stirred up about running the ball successfully into the sixth green at the Old Course, perhaps hitting a one-hundred-yard punch shot under the wind; and I might not feel a rush of adrenalin when I tee it up on the long par-five fourteenth, with its area of fairway known as the Elysian Fields out there for me to find; nor will I feel instantly calmed when I find the right spot on the fairway. The penalties for missing aren't so obvious or final, nor are the rewards so apparent. But a sense of accomplishment builds when I play the proper shots. A well-played series of shots at classic courses brings a glow that lasts.

Crenshaw is well aware of the contrasting pleasures between classic and modern courses. He's studied course architecture. He's read the classics, including MacKenzie's 1920 book, *Golf Architecture*, and Charles Blair Macdonald's 1928 study, *Scotland's Gift, Golf*. He's visited many of the classic courses and once led a tour to the historic courses of Scotland and England with writer Herbert Warren Wind. Crenshaw has also written his own afterword to a reprint of Bernard Darwin's 1910 classic, *The Golf Courses of the British Isles*.

"Every serious study or article on golf-course architecture," Crenshaw writes, "all the way back to Old Tom Morris (one of its first practitioners) has grasped the cardinal principles of strategic golf-course design but, strangely enough, these principles are not understood as clearly today."

Crenshaw might as well have been beside me as I stood over my forty-yard shot to Worlington's first green. Even here I have choices. I can run the ball into the green or I can carry it on. There's no intervening sand trap. It's up to me. This is what golf should be like, an alternative to having everything done for us. Too many modern golf courses leave us little choice. They're contrived, because an architect can do anything with modern earth-moving equipment. He can zap the land. I agree with Crenshaw's idea that courses should appear to be entirely natural, where the holes fit the terrain. Some modern architects haven't even visited the British courses that stand up so well. How can they call themselves architects? Would a classical musician never have studied Bach? Crenshaw knows better. He's taking up course architecture, and I look forward to his work. He knows that it's enlightening to consider the past, to learn from past masters.

My choice, then. I decide to hit a little bump and run onto the first green. The green slopes away from me as I look at it, and I don't want to risk putting the ball in the air and landing short, or worse, too far on the right side of the green where the ball will kick off. Wouldn't you know it, though, I suddenly feel that I might shank the shot. A shank is the worst shot a golfer can hit. It's terrifying, the ball jumping crazily off the hosel of the clubhead and skittering off to the side at a bizarre angle. I'd had such a thought while standing on the first tee during the 1977 British Amateur championship at the Ganton Golf Club in Yorkshire, England. A hedge was on the right of the tee, and as I stood on the tee I envisaged my ball careening off my club into the hedge. I couldn't possibly hit a shot so poorly, or could I? I laughed at my ridiculous thought and stepped away, then hit a good drive.

But what happens when even stepping away doesn't help? What happens when you do everything right and still the clamorous nervous system takes over? That's why there's a psychology of golf. That's why every nineteenth hole at every golf course is full of golf philosophers.

I know that it was silly of me to worry about a shank as I played my approach on Worlington's opening hole. But that didn't help; I still felt the way I did. Yet I also knew that it wouldn't matter even if I did shank. Golfers at all levels, even Crenshaw's, have suffered every indignity the game has to offer, and under public scrutiny. But that's part of golf. You can't control the game or yourself, not all the time.

In the end, I calm down and realize that my pitch shot is just another shot. It doesn't have to be such an effort. Letting go of anxiety allows me to feel the swing I want to make; the result proves that relaxation is important. My ball pitches near the front of the green and finishes ten feet from the hole. I miss the putt, but I've played a decent first hole. I'd played the hole intelligently, made one mistake that wasn't too serious when I pushed my three-wood slightly, and then quieted my nerves to play the pitch into the green.

My first hole sets me up for the round at Worlington. I'm in control most of the nine holes and very aware of the environment. I'm playing well, inspired by the glorious day, the fine old course, and the memories of certain conversations I'd had with Crenshaw. I can see him at Worlington, hitting a variety of shots. He belongs here.

Crenshaw would really show his class on the par-three fifth hole, a 157-yarder where the tee shot has to carry a corner of the fourth

green and also part of the walk from the sixth tee to the sixth fairway. Nobody would build a hole like this today, but it has its own
charm and requires only that golfers be courteous. That's the way
the land lies, that's the way the hole will be. The fifth also happens
to be a splendid par-three; a long hogback green falls off on either
side. The pin today is on the rear, high portion of the green. The
wind is blowing now, left to right and into my face.

This is some hole. It's got everything — a natural feel, an interesting green, trouble if you miss the green, but not so much that
you can't play a shot and save your par. Then there's that feeling
of openness that we always come back to. No doubt Crenshaw
would hit a shot directly into that openness — the heart of the green,
that is — and let his ball skip to the back section. I tried to hit a
similar shot, but some fear in the back of my mind gnawed at me
just as I took the club back. I didn't want to miss the green to the
right, down a hill, so I overprotected and hit the ball left. It wasn't
a bad shot, as it did catch a corner of the green. But it demonstrated
the importance of concentrating on where I wanted the ball to go.
Instead, I was emphasizing where I'd rather it didn't go.

I wasn't satisfied with the shot, but I had to go on. Happily, it
was easy to forget the shot. There was so much else to catch my
eye. First, naturally, was that openness, which meant that the game
changed so much from day to day. Nothing happens the same way
on the best courses, and British courses in particular usually play
fast; that is, the ground is firm. The wind blows. The ball bounces.
You have to play many kinds of shots. Golf becomes a ground game
as well as a game played through the air.

One reason for this is that British courses aren't watered to the
extent North American courses are. Crenshaw had talked to me
about this. "I think the courses in America are overwatered," he
said. "Golf is a soft game here. And I might add that in the next
ten years we are going to have to use much less water in America.
We have a serious water shortage, and we are going to see courses
with less land to maintain, much less water. So if you combine the
idea of a fast course that stimulates shot-making with the current
high maintenance costs for watering, you begin to feel golf may
become more of a shot-maker's game again."

Golf is a shot-maker's game at Royal Worlington. Worlington's nine holes stimulated my golfing mind. I took notes on many subjects: swing technique, the psychology of the game, its literature, courses and personalities, the lure of the links. The course has had its effect. I'm spellbound by the warmth the game can bring. I'm ready to write about the dimensions of the game, to consider in detail its many facets, why it's more of an obsession than a hobby for many participants, whether they play at my Highway Hideaway Golf Course, Augusta National, or Royal Worlington and Newmarket.

# To Have and Have Not:
## In Search of the Swing

The golf swing is an arcane motion, as difficult to produce on demand as the correct pirouette in a figure skater's routine. Properly performed, it combines rhythm, tempo, and mechanics in a pleasing way. Each alone provides some degree of efficiency, but to study each alone is to risk losing the others. Yet to study the aspects as a group is to risk losing oneself in endless permutations and combinations, many of which work some of the time, and in their own time.

The swing is to some degree ineffable, which is exactly the reason so many golfers try to explain it. Typically, we try to understand what went right that last swing; we break the swing down into movements, then concentrate on what we think worked — the left hip sliding out of the way just so as we moved from the top of the swing back toward the ball, perhaps. Focus on that, however, and we lose something else. The swing is a whole, but we try to understand it in parts. Neither vertical nor horizontal in plane, neither all arms and hands nor all back and shoulders, the swing is . . . what? How are we to know it?

We can ask teachers. A massive industry is in place to help golfers improve, but there is so little consistency from one teacher to another as to render the search for a better swing apparently hopeless. Typically, a golfer will improve shortly after taking a lesson, the principle being that he now has something to think about. But every golfer knows how quickly he reverts to form. His rooted way of swinging the club asserts itself. Indeed the golf swing seems as personal as a signature, and as resistant to change. I can identify a friend as much by his swing from 100 yards away as by his voice over the phone.

Nobody has really figured out what makes the swing work and what makes it come apart, or, more important, how to help golfers learn. Endless theories present themselves, creating migraines for golfers and small fortunes for instructors. Byron Nelson wrote that golf is a left-sided game for right-handers. Seve Ballesteros argues for the right side. Lanny Wadkins's swing suggests that fast hands and active wrists are essential. Curtis Strange's swing indicates that hands and wrists have little or no place in the swing; the big muscles of the back and legs matter. Bobby Jones wrote that the golfer must be comfortable and feel natural over the ball, and that he should never give up these feelings, even in the interest of swing thoughts that might make him more efficient. Ben Hogan wrote that golf isn't a natural game at all, and that anybody who cared to improve had better learn the right moves.

Scientists have grappled with the golf swing, perhaps because it lends itself to analysis. Writer Paul Gallico called golf "a mystery as much of a one as the universe and solar systems, electricity or ionic affinities." Gallico must have written these words after having examined his swing problems and then having gone through every checklist of swing mechanics that he knew. No doubt he set up in the proper manner to the ball and then hit it into the raspberry bushes, thereby prompting the question, "How can I ever figure this game out?" Golf scientists are guided by the same missionary zeal.

The first golf scientist to make himself known was one Thomas

Kincaid, an Edinburgh medical student and beginner golfer. Having returned from the course on January 20, 1687, Kincaid wrote in his diary, probably with a dram of medicinal whiskey at his side: "After dinner I went out to the golve. . . . I found the only way of playing at the golve is: 1, to stand as you do at fencing with a small sword, bending your legs a little, and holding the muscles of your legs and back and armes exceeding bent or fixt or stiffe, and not at all slackening them in the time you are bringing down the stroak."

History does not record whether Kincaid's musings led him to any championships, but we do know that his thoughts represent the first known recorded words of golf analysis and instruction. Centuries later the flow of information continues, an avalanche of golf theory. The most comprehensive analysis of the swing yet undertaken was conducted by the Golf Society of Great Britain, during the 1960s. The Society resulted from the passion of Australian Sir Aynsley Bridgland, a civil engineer who in 1929 moved to England where he made his way in real estate. Bridgland always said he wished to fulfill three main objectives: to own a Rolls-Royce, to become a millionaire, and to reduce his handicap to scratch. He managed all three and was the happiest for achieving the latter goal. But his greatest accomplishment may well turn out to be his role in the founding of the GSGB, a group comprising some ten scientists whose purpose was to study the principles of the golf swing. The group included experts in ballistics, anatomy, ergonomics, physiology, biomechanics, anatomy, and physics.

The GSGB published its findings in 1968, in *The Search for the Perfect Swing*. The volume is fascinating, full of information on the science of the swing. We learn, for example, that the golf ball is in contact with the clubhead for less than half a millisecond, and that it takes twenty times that brief time span for the golfer to feel in his fingers what he has just done. The scientists make it very plain that we therefore do not feel what happens when we hit the ball, but only what happens after we have hit it. Moreover, the golfer can do nothing, absolutely nothing, about how he hits the ball once he has started his downswing. It's out of his hands, so to speak. Yet Jack Nicklaus, for one, claims he can compensate for a poor beginning to his downswing by some maneuver. I'm not one to argue with Nicklaus, but research suggests there's no physiological basis for what he says he can do.

*The Search for the Perfect Swing* makes no claims to being an instruction book, but it does arrive at a model of the ideal swing. Unfortunately, as the authors point out, there is a gap between the ideal and what a human being can achieve. Wrist movement during the swing, for example, is complex and best served by a grip that permits free hinging of the wrists. But that happens only when the golfer holds the club loosely in his left hand, or places his right hand on top of the left. Conversely, the model suggests we should place our hands apart if we are to maximize leverage during the swing. The grip is, in the end, a compromise.

Other models besides the GSGB's exist. Ralph Mann, a former U.S. Olympic silver medalist in track and field who holds a doctorate in biomechanics, analyzed the performance of fifty-four PGA Tour pros. Mann feels that the top golfers set ideal, universal standards. They should be our models. He hoped that he could match an amateur's swing characteristics to those of a pro of similar physical stature. The amateur could then try to model his swing after the pro's.

Mann's contingent included Nicklaus, Greg Norman, Arnold Palmer, Ben Crenshaw, and Tom Watson. The scientist, based in Orlando, Florida, calls these fellows the "chief executive officers of their swings," because they have been through his computer analysis and have access to reams of data that they can study and that relate to all aspects of their swings. But even they sometimes measure up wrong against the ideal model for their build and height. "Norman made significant changes in his swing after being measured against the ideal model," Mann told me one winter day in his lab. "He went from standing upright to a more flexed position over the ball."

The data that Mann came up with suggest that most golfers swing too slowly. This is startling information, but it made sense when I heard it from Mann. "Everyone wants you to swing back slow and smooth," he said. "But the slower you go, the more chance you have to manipulate the club."

I don't know. The more I think about the scientific approach to golf, the less capable I seem of swinging the club with any grace. It sometimes seems impossible to reconcile the need for information with the desire simply to play the game, to swing away. At the same time, we all want to improve.

I believe in a long-term approach to learning the proper fundamentals of the swing. This is because I've tried the short-term, Band-Aid approaches. Magazine "tips" don't work as long-term remedies for faulty swings. Glitches reoccur, hence my advocacy of the long-term view. I can allow for the inevitable mistakes and assign them to human nature.

The nature of the game itself makes it next to impossible to perform well consistently. Canadian touring pro Dan Halldorson once stood on the tee of the 197-yard par-three seventh hole at the Glen Abbey Golf Club, the permanent site of the Canadian Open, and commented, "It's ridiculous, isn't it? Here's this ball, and there's the hole, 4¼" in diameter. We're expected to get the ball from here to there in three shots, across all this land and water. And what's more amazing, sometimes we do it in one shot. It boggles the mind to even think about it."

In that statement, Halldorson articulated the absurdity of the game. Toward that end golfers have written thousands of instructional articles and books. Glossy magazines make millions of dollars because their readers crave the newest, the latest, the hottest theory, or, more accurately, the latest tip. An editor of one of the major U.S. publications told me with more than a hint of snarling pleasure in his voice that once a year his magazine runs an instructional article that is intended to confound readers, the better to bring them back for the next issue.

Let's be certain. We humans are complex beings, and we become excessively complex with a golf club in our hands. Yet our only chance is to think things through, for, as Ben Hogan himself said, golf can't be taught, it can only be learned. He meant that we have to find our own way, given a few salient pointers. Hogan was an optimist. He wrote the following in his book, *The Modern Fundamentals of Golf,* published in 1957: "Up to a considerable point, as I see it, there's nothing difficult about golf, nothing. I see no reason, truly, why the average golfer, if he goes about it intelligently, shouldn't play in the seventies — and I mean by playing the type of shots a fine golfer plays."

I love those words. I read them every spring and am full of hope. But by July I've realized again that it's impossible to learn golf from a book alone. You have to see somebody, and then get to work.

Golf shouldn't be so tough. After all, nobody is smashing a ball at you, as in tennis. You aren't asked to drive an automobile that looks like a spaceship around hairpin turns at speeds that can exceed 200 miles per hour. Nobody is whipping a ball at you at nearly 100 miles per hour, as in baseball. You aren't balancing on thin blades while hurtling along ice toward a net. All you're doing in golf is standing still, with an implement in your hands created specifically for the task, trying to advance a ball — also resting in place — toward a clearly evident target, and with nobody protecting it. And you've got fourteen such implements at your disposal. What's the problem?

The problem is that the object of attention — the ball — is stationary. So are you. Unlike hockey, football, tennis, soccer, Ping-Pong or badminton, golf is a game not of reaction, but of creation. Don Edwards, an excellent goalkeeper for the Buffalo Sabres of the National Hockey League during the late 1970s and a low-handicap golfer, says that he can understand hockey because he reflexively moves to where the puck is; but golf mystifies him. What, he wonders, makes a golfer take the club back? There the ball sits, at the golfer's feet, waiting to be struck. Its resting position invites him to hit it, taunting him, teasing him, suggesting that he, and only he, has total control over its flight. No wonder tennis whiz Ivan Lendl is captivated by golf, though by the end of 1988 he was still stuck on a ten-handicap. He had thoughts of a much lower handicap, because he figured he could understand the swing and make it happen. Chicago Bulls' basketball star Michael Jordan has said that he wants to become a pro golfer after he's through with basketball. Surely, he suggested, the swing can be mastered. It's easy, compared to basketball. All you have to do is swing. But how? How can you swing when the ball is still? What makes you swing? We know, after all, that such sports as tennis and baseball present the most difficulty precisely when the athlete must initiate a motion, rather than react. Tennis players become paralyzed while trying to come up with a better serve — the only time in the game that the ball is at rest. Baseball pitchers have the toughest assignment in their sport, also because they start with a ball at rest.

I think I know the problem. I've hit enough decent shots in my life to have glimpsed golfing heaven: the well-struck shot that comes off exactly as I planned it. I know that I can hit at least one shot a round as well as Nicklaus or any other champion who has ever played the game. We all have a little of the Ben Hogan in our golf game. You *can* control the flight of the golf ball from time to time. You may never be able to return Boris Becker's serve, but you can play a hole with Greg Norman and even beat him that hole, with well-struck shots. It can happen. We all have it in us. Where exactly is the problem?

Unfortunately, you also see the possibility of failure every time you look at the ball, sitting there so innocuously. Your pain is assured. So is the illusion — or the belief — that you can succeed. The only way to play the game is to play it one shot at a time. Every shot offers the possibility of success, of immediate reward. And every shot offers the possibility of failure as well. It mixes a player up. But it also mixes up Hogan and Nicklaus. I caddied for Jim Nelford during the 1980 Canadian Open at Royal Montreal Golf Club, and Nicklaus was in the group. He faced a pitch shot from thirty yards to an open green. There was nothing to it, and Nicklaus showed no indication of worry. But he hit the shot fat, moving it maybe ten yards and then shook his head as if to say, "That's golf." He approached the ball again, and this time put it up near the hole. It was as if a writer suddenly did not know how to write a sentence with a subject and verb in it; indeed, that he had no conception of how to do so. A moment later, though, it all came back to him.

Hogan claimed he hit but one or two shots a round that came off exactly as he intended. Nicklaus has said he has not come near the perfect game. We all know what we want to do with the ball when we arrange ourselves around it, but that knowledge is not enough. Will is not enough. We need to understand the fundamentals of the swing, at the very least, and then get to work. We need to know the golf swing, to have a sound grounding in the basics. We need to know what works and how to apply it. Hogan and Nicklaus surely know the fundamentals, but even they have difficulty applying them. As for me, I played golf the first twenty years or so by feel alone. I didn't think fundamentals were important. But then I woke up and craved more consistency in my game. I'd listened to and read enough tips and I wanted to take a long-term approach to improvement. I was ready to learn.

February 1985. I'm heading for the Frenchman's Creek Golf Club in North Palm Beach, Florida. I have an appointment with Jack Grout, who was then seventy-one. He was the head pro in 1950 at the Scioto Country Club in Columbus, Ohio, when he encountered ten-year-old Jack Nicklaus in a morning junior clinic. Nicklaus worked with Grout until the fine teacher's death in May 1989.

   Grout, a lanky man who was so at ease with himself that he could be at home anywhere, recognized rare qualities in the young Nicklaus. Nicklaus worked harder than any other youngster in the clinic, and before long Grout was asking him to demonstrate certain fundamentals. Grout taught fundamentals, which is one reason I've come to see him. I don't want a complex approach to the game. I'm looking for something I can work with for years, a concept of the swing that is grounded in common sense and that I can believe in. "The fundamentals don't change," Nicklaus once told me. "They're the same today as when I began."

   Driving into Frenchman's Creek, I spot Grout. He's sitting in a golf cart on the practice range, chin in his left hand. Grout is watching Richard Leconch, a young, burly pro from Connecticut. Grout and Nicklaus have recently gotten together for their annual "state-of-Jack's-game" review. It takes place at the beginning of the season, or anytime during the season when Nicklaus is in need. Nicklaus calls their first meeting of the year his annual checkup, when Grout goes over the game from the grip onward. You'd think Nicklaus wouldn't forget these things from one winter to the next, but there you have it.

First, I watch. Grout notices that Leconch is taking deep divots with a wedge. Something's wrong. Leconch then moves on to two-irons.

"Is the face of the club square?" Grout asks Leconch. "Square the face of the club up. Utilize your swing and hit it." Grout gave similar advice to the youthful Nicklaus when he told him to hit the ball hard and worry about swing mechanics later. But Leconch is a man, not a boy. His moves are ingrained habits. How can he stop thinking and just hit the ball, especially when it's just sitting there? Predictably, he can't. He keeps asking questions of his teacher. "Is my ball position all right?" Grout tells him it's fine, that it's sound policy to play the ball off the heel of one's forward foot for all conventional shots. He's advocating something that could help in achieving that Holy Grail of consistency.

Grout continues. "Do you like to practice?" he asks Leconch. "I love to practice."

"Well, now you have something to work on to your benefit."

Leconch listens, all the while making what seem to be fine swings, if the flight of the ball is any criterion. Not surprisingly, he's ecstatic.

"Jack," he says, excitedly, "if I could hit the ball like this all the time . . . well, it's up to me, what I want to do with it."

"It's practice," Grout tells his pupil, "and confidence. You've got the swing and you've got the ball position. I don't see how you can miss it from there."

But I wonder. Golfers do miss it from there. Nicklaus believes that setup, or address, is ninety percent of golf. In my time I've worked hard on setup — though I may have been setting up wrong — and swung through to what I thought was an ideal finishing position, facing the target, head held high, eyes forward, in balance. Yet the ball has often gone awry. The fundamentals of position are important, but ninety percent?

It's my turn now. But Grout wants to talk with me before watching me hit balls. As much good can come from chatting with a teacher as in going out on the practice range or course. I need a comprehensive theory that will help me understand the swing. I need a philosophy of the game, a way into it. I won't get that while standing on the range in front of Grout. Chances are that I'll get too nervous.

Grout tells me he's going to keep it simple. That I like. Just the basics, nothing fancy. He's heard all the fancy theories and he knows I've heard them. He'd like me to rid my golfing mind of them. "Look," he says. "I watch pros teach sometimes and it just turns my stomach. They diagnose poorly because they don't have enough experience. If they did, they wouldn't say those crazy things. Instead of leaving well enough alone and sticking with fundamentals, they gotta come up with something new. Look here, I keep telling people. Don't always listen to what they're telling you. You're not learning how to dig a ditch. You're learning how to swing a golf club."

How did Nicklaus learn to swing a golf club? That's the question I ask of Grout. Was it natural talent? A gift?

"Jack started at age ten, with dedication. At sixteen he won the Ohio Open, beating some fine pros and amateurs. That was when I knew he had it. It takes five years to learn this game, five years for things to sink in. Most people want Band-Aids. They don't want to take the time." Of course, as Grout points out almost as an aside, Nicklaus had something else. "Some people are here to do something," Grout tells me. "Jack was born to be a great player. He's got a brilliant mind. He can figure out complicated things for himself." It also helps that Nicklaus thrived on practicing. Grout remembers an afternoon when Nicklaus, bundled up in a rain suit, hit balls for two hours at Frenchman's Creek during a deluge, while Grout and pro Gardner Dickinson watched from under an umbrella.

As always, I find such talk inspiring. To visit with a teacher is to hang on to his every word. Something will register. Some of the ideas will get through. Something will fit and I'll become the player I can be. I listen, and then I hear it. "The longer you play with good fundamentals," Grout says, "you just keep on improving." That is, you can't just play by feel. I had done so for too long, but the feel I had was disordered, connections I made randomly while over the ball. Why was it that when I stood over a shot I needed to hook, suddenly I often felt my swing cutting across the ball, producing a slice? It didn't happen all the time, but it was disquieting when it did. Why couldn't I decide whether the right way for a tall golfer like me to play was with an upright swing or a flat swing? I looked at George Archer, 6′5″, and saw a successful player who stooped over the ball. I looked at Tom Weiskopf, the 6′3″ owner of a most gracious swing, and saw a gifted player who stood nearly to his height at the ball. I had hit decent shots and horrible shots both ways. And what about extension through the ball? Once, while leading a club championship, I had tried to emulate Trevino by driving through the ball with my legs, arms extended to the target. I felt rigid, forced, and caught the middle of the ball with the bottom edge of my clubhead. The cut ball tore through the green, and my chances of winning went with it. What was I trying to do, anyway?

One bad swing at the wrong time — just like that — can produce fear for months, or years. Johnny Miller had once shanked a shot on national television while playing Pebble Beach Golf Links in Monterey, California. He said he feared shanking every short iron he set up to for the next year. Ballesteros missed a six-foot par putt that would have kept him in a play-off for the 1987 Masters. He didn't regain his confidence until more than a year later, when he won the 1988 British Open at Royal Lytham & St. Annes in England. Misery lodges in the golfing mind; the nature of the game — that stationary ball again — gives us time to think. Memories bubble forth; amateurs have years of unpleasant memories of golf balls going every which way but the one they wanted. Pros remember the one bad swing, not the many good ones. Feel? I had too much of it, I thought, too much, anyway, that wasn't connected to sound mechanics. Alone with Jack Grout on a muggy day in Florida, the range all ours, I needed to learn the mechanics. And, of course, something more. But that would be a beginning.

The lesson went well. Grout was a wise tutor from the start. He encouraged me to believe in my swing, because he thought it wasn't far from being of sound construction. It had flow, pace, and rhythm. But I used my hands too much. The clubhead moved around, and I depended on timing to get it back squarely to the ball. Grout showed me how to reduce the activity of my hands without losing the feel that was so much a part of my swing.

"Just turn your shoulders," he advised, standing opposite me. "I want to see your right shoulder at the top of your swing. The idea is to use all of yourself. That's what you need to do. You're cutting your motion off. Let yourself turn so that your back faces the target at the top of the swing. That'll give you a full arc."

Grout then went into the basics, things I should try to achieve on each shot but that weren't unique to my game. We worked on six components of all fine swings: grip, setup, a steady head, footwork, full extension, and "quiet" (passive) hands. These six, when integrated effectively, accomplish what pros consider to be the objectives of the swing, "power with direction, direction with power."

The golf swing, Grout told me, is a means of building energy on the backswing and releasing it on the downswing, culminating in that firecracker sound of club meeting ball that all golfers cherish. I'd heard that sound from time to time in my own game. But it happened by chance. I wanted it to happen because of solid mechanics.

Too many golfers, Grout told me, short-change the pre-swing fundamentals of grip and setup. Others never generate any *potential* energy on their backswings; they're prone to picking the club up with their hands and arms without using the muscles in their legs and back. And even those golfers who do create some energy going back often dissipate it before they get to the ball. Afraid they might not contact the ball properly, they cast the club with their hands from the top of their swing. "Gone fishing," they might say. They never generate any energy, thus have nothing to unleash. Grout counteracts these tendencies by drilling into his students early on his concept of the swing as a build-up and release of energy.

Then the professor of the swing moves to the grip. A player's hands, he notes, are his only connection to the club. Better start there, then. "You can't overcome a poor grip," Grout tells me, and he'll tell it to me again and again. "If your hands are situated on the shaft wrong, that makes the game more difficult to begin with. A bad grip disrupts a good swing." That is, a golfer can't expect to play well consistently with a poor grip. How misguided, then, that so many of us use grips more suited to changing a tire than swinging a golf club. It's particularly absurd when you think that the grip is one fundamental we can control. We might be able to forgive the problems we have once we set the club in motion; it goes off on its own track. But why start with a poor grip?

Grout advocates the palms-opposed grip. The right palm (for a right-hander) faces the target, while the left palm, on the other side of the clubshaft, faces the right palm from slightly above. This enables the left wrist to face the target at address. It previews the desired position at impact, when the left wrist again faces the target. Clubhead control is the goal. It's essential to the repeating, efficient swing.

To unite the hands, Grout suggests I take up what has become known as the Vardon, or overlapping grip. (This is in honor of Harry Vardon, who didn't invent the grip, but who made it famous while using it for his six British Open victories.) The right hand folds over the left, its little finger overlapping the area between the index and middle fingers of the left hand. This gets the two hands working as one. "You don't want slippage," Grout says. Should a golfer's hands be smaller than average, he can vary the Vardon grip so the little finger of the right hand is placed between the middle and index fingers on the left, interlocking with the latter. Then again, there's the ten-finger baseball grip, favored by touring pro Dave Barr. His colleagues call him Hands, because he seems to guide his golf club through the air like a conductor leads an orchestra, all motion and twisty movements. If you don't like the overlapping grip, the interlocking grip, or the ten-finger baseball grip, try pro Ed Fiori's grip. A right-handed golfer, he places his left hand on the club so that his wrist is almost facing the sky. His right hand is almost under the clubshaft. He's not the world's greatest golfer, but he has won more than a million dollars on the PGA Tour, as well as three tournaments through 1989. His nickname on Tour? The Grip. What else? But the way he holds a club isn't recommended.

I decide to use the conventional overlapping grip. It feels good and it makes sense. It's also one less thing to worry about. I can reduce the clutter in my mind if I take care of this before I swing.

Now, Grout says, I should concern myself with my target. It's all part of the setup. It means aiming the clubface from behind the ball toward the target, then positioning my body parallel to that line, since I'm standing to one side of the ball. That, too, makes sense; if I were driving from New York to Boston, I wouldn't aim my car toward Toronto, would I? Not unless I wanted to take some detours, and maybe never reach my destination. Yet we golfers often aim our clubfaces and our bodies at bizarre angles to our targets. Maybe we don't want to get there. Or maybe we've never taken the time to learn how to aim properly. Grout says that barely five percent of golfers aim correctly. It seems amazing.

"It's hard to hit a good shot from poor alignment," he advises. "You have to make compensations during your swing." But that introduces more sources of error. Better to get my feet, hips, and shoulders set up properly from the beginning.

Nobody lines up more methodically than Nicklaus. At Loxahatchee, a course that he designed not far from his home in Lost Tree Village, Florida, and where he practices, I watched as he set up carefully on each shot. It didn't matter that he was just practicing rather than playing in a tournament. He works on each and every shot, be it for a Masters championship or for a late-evening round with his children at Loxahatchee. It's as if he thinks he'll pay later if he doesn't pay attention now. I have never seen him play a shot carelessly. There he is, putting the club behind the ball, then aligning his feet and body, always checking his location by swiveling his eyes forward to a spot a few inches in front of the ball, then a few feet, and finally, all the way to his target.

There's more to the pre-swing routine than grip and alignment. The golfer needs to maintain good posture. With the spine straight, hands hanging from his body, he's in what San Diego teacher Ed Roscoe calls an apelike position. He's slightly bent over so that he can get his club behind the ball, but the general appearance is of comfort and ease. He's in a go position.

This position is enhanced, Grout says, when I keep my head steady while swinging. I hear him, and I know that Nicklaus keeps his head steady, but I'm also aware that George Knudson — acknowledged by Nicklaus himself to be one of the great ball-strikers in golf —

did not believe the head should remain still. That restricts freedom, Dr. George used to say, and freedom is what you want in the golf swing. No restrictions. Just let it loose. The head goes where the body goes. The body moves on the backswing; so should the head. Otherwise you're frozen.

Grout explains his position, or rather, the head's position. "I don't mean to say you lock your head in one position," he says. "You have to be comfortable. But it's pretty close to that. Your head is the center of your balance." Balance is also a main element in Knudson's teachings. "Never do anything at the expense of balance," he always said. He argues that balance is enhanced when the head moves. Grout argues that head motion destroys balance. I think they're talking about the same thing; Nicklaus's head isn't as rigid as he suggests, and Knudson's was steadier than he felt.

Grout, Knudson, and other teachers do agree on what constitutes balance. They mean an element common to all graceful motion, be it the sweep of a ballerina, the acceleration of a hockey player, the windup of a pitcher. Should the golfer's head move mid-swing, Grout argues, he will sway. His swing will be thrown off track, and he's liable to nearly fall off his feet during the follow-through. The likely result is a dramatic loss of potential power and direction.

Grout suggests that golfers looking for consistency adopt a move similar to the one that has become a Nicklaus trademark. He first addresses the ball with his head slightly behind it, then cocks his chin to his right, effectively setting it there. In so doing, he knows exactly where his head is as he swings back and through — he's done something to put it there. His steady head locates him in space. It is *the* orienting principle.

Now, finally, the swing itself comes into play and I generate the energy that I then release. It feels good, too, turning my back to the target, fully wound up, coiled, and then springing back to and through the ball. Sam Snead said he liked to feel "oily" when he swung the club. Gene Sarazen, the winner of the 1935 Masters, said he liked to feel as if he were riding through the ball. I like these images. Swept away and along by energy I've created on the back-swing, I feel propelled on the downswing and through the ball. Golf becomes physically satisfying, but only after I have begun to understand it intellectually. The mind first, then the muscles. Then, I hope, the two together on the course, for more than one swing at a time.

But how am I to activate all this motion? Grout lets me in on his secrets: full extension and proper footwork, fundamentals four and five. When these work together, I'm stretched and wound to my limit at the top of my swing. I'm ready to unload the energy that I've gathered to that point. Yet I'm not, significantly, in a hurry. I wait, and my downswing and throughswing happen, or so they should.

I achieve full extension when I turn my hips and shoulders as much as possible without losing balance. The shaft of my club then points toward my target. Standing opposite me, Grout will now be able to see my right shoulder blade at the top of my swing, as long as I've turned smoothly ninety degrees from my address position. Ben Hogan knew he did so when he felt his left shoulder hitting his chin as he turned away from the ball; his shirts were worn thin at that point. My chin doesn't rub against my left shoulder. My backswing has generally been a choppy affair in which I've picked up the club and flicked it back. I've often gotten away with it because of good timing and rhythm; it's also hurt me when the feel wasn't there. Then I needed sound mechanics, but I had no foundation. Maybe, just maybe, though, I'm on my way. At least Grout hasn't suggested I leave the range, and he doesn't seem exasperated. My shots are flying long and straight. Life is good.

I now learn another important point: Extension is impossible without good footwork. On my backswing, I need to roll my left ankle inward toward the inside of my right foot, transferring my weight along the way. From the top of my swing, stretched taut as a bow, I'm to roll my right ankle back toward my left, returning my weight toward that side. Nicklaus did this hundreds of times a day as a kid, just standing in place, rolling his ankles. He calls this "playing from the insides of my feet." It's not something amateurs usually look for when watching the pros. But proper footwork, when integrated with the hip and shoulder turn, promotes the build-up and release of energy. And it seems simple while Grout is with me. I'm feeling like a golfer, a real golfer, one whose body is in control and one who can control the flight of the golf ball. Nevertheless, I'm not done. One more fundamental to learn.

Fundamental number six is straightforward: Keep the hands quiet during the swing. Don't let them flutter, twist, or run off on their own. Let the motion of the swing carry them. It's all in the service of a full arc, that guarantor of consistency. If the arc, or the distance the clubhead travels, is the same every time, then a source of error is eliminated. And it all begins with keeping the left arm straight, but not rigid. Should the left arm break down, the arc will shorten; so too will the distance the ball travels. Short, choppy arcs don't create much clubhead speed. It's important to let the club gather momentum along a full arc; a car that accelerates over two blocks will reach a higher speed than the car that accelerates over one block. Apply that principle to clubhead speed and you're on your way to realizing why a full arc is important. Understand full extension, Grout suggests, and don't allow the left arm to collapse. A straight left arm ensures a consistent swing radius; the more I do it, the more I know what it is, the more I'll learn to feel it. Then I can correct it whenever necessary. Quiet hands go a long way toward producing the full arc.

Quiet hands also ensure that I'll return the clubhead to the ball square to my target. My left wrist will be flat, unbent as at address. My hands will have flowed through to the position previewed at address. The club will flow rather than flail because I have allowed what is known as clubhead lag or clubhead delay to be created during my downswing.

The action is similar to a baseball pitcher's motion as he goes forward from the top of his windup: His weight shifts to his front foot; then his arm, hand, and following leg come forward, releasing the ball almost without his throwing it. It's as if the pitcher surrenders the ball. It's all he can do, and it's all set up by what came before. Otherwise he could only flick the ball with little power or direction.

In golf it all comes to a head at the ball. There the accumulated energy is let loose. The clubhead explodes through the ball at impact, carrying me, a right-handed golfer, to a finishing position with all my weight on my left foot. My torso is facing my target, in balance. Best of all, with the pieces assembled, it feels easy and effortless.

This all takes time before it becomes a habit. I'm not certain it ever becomes second nature. Nicklaus says he falls into bad habits, but can usually get himself out in a day or two. Watson also loses the flow of his swing periodically and even seemed to lose it for good during the late 1980s, when he admitted that he just didn't have much of a game. "When I'm having trouble," he had told me in 1980, when he was challenging Nicklaus as the best golfer of the time, "my swing doesn't stay together. It becomes a series of pieces. I take the club back too much with my hands. My right side stays too high. It's not a flowing motion." Watson knew all this, but he could not make himself improve. He saw his long-time instructor Byron Nelson, and he went for a make-over to David Leadbetter, a Florida-based teaching pro who revamped Englishman Nick Faldo's swing over a two-year period starting in 1984. Faldo had said to Leadbetter then, "Throw the book at me." Faldo went on to win the 1987 British Open and the 1989 Masters. But Watson, a few years older, with more failures and more recent poor swings to reckon with, was still struggling. It was nearly impossible to detect what was wrong in his swing, but that didn't stop him, or Leadbetter, from trying. I watched Watson during the 1989 Masters and the 1989 U.S. Open at Rochester's Oak Hill club. Except for a few errant shots, a few swings that weren't aggressive through the ball, à la Watson of old, there wasn't much to suggest why he was troubled. He knew the fundamentals of the swing, but he couldn't put them together. Something was missing. Watson was trying to find it, whatever "it" is.

Golfers around the world, myself included, are also trying to find our swings. We're learning slowly. Grout offered me possibility and hope, grounded in reasonableness. He offered a flowing motion by which I could enjoy golf, shot by shot, hole by hole, round by round.

Grout was Nicklaus's primary instructor; in his will his last bequest was to his protégé. "To Jack Nicklaus," he wrote, "I give my thanks." Nicklaus also thanks Grout. J. Grout, as Nicklaus called him, helped the youngster become a legend. J. Grout is a legend in his own right for knowing and being able to communicate the fundamentals of the golf swing.

After seeing Grout, I realized that the pleasures of the game were all ahead of me. I didn't get to know him very well, but I did have that not-to-be-forgotten morning with him at Frenchman's Creek. He helped me realize that sense can be made of the golf swing. After working with Grout, I worked on a book with George Knudson. He amplified my thinking and showed me that the golf swing did not have to be complicated. Sure, there's much more to scoring well than understanding the swing, but it's a sensible beginning.

I think I'm beginning to understand the swing. My mentors have offered me a sound program for advancement. This doesn't mean I will look the same as others who have learned from them. Not at all. As Grout told me, Lee Trevino's swing works pretty well, even though it looks like what he calls "junkyard dog." But check Trevino's fundamentals. They're all there.

After nearly thirty years of golf, then, I don't mind what Grout emphasized. "It takes five hard, strenuous years to learn the game, but with continuous practice and concentration, the fundamentals become integrated into a package." That's encouraging. I'll find the time. I'll consider the fundamentals and accept that things won't always go well. I'll think about what went right, not what went wrong. I'll concentrate on the good, gradually eliminating the bad. I'll maintain good faith. I'll practice.

Building a golf swing has come down to this for me: Golf is a lifelong game, so why not stick to the basics, grooving them day after day? A solid golf swing grounded in fundamentals is possible. It just takes time. Golf offers plenty of that.

# THREE

# Mind Games

Cypress Point in Monterey, California, is golf's most aesthetically pleasing course. Situated high on a hill above the Pacific coast, it is stunning in its setting. The course tumbles from a high first tee with the coastline spread beneath, then moves into dense forest before breaking into sand hills and on to the renowned sixteenth hole, a 233-yard par-three that plays across an inlet to a green set on a peninsula. Rocks, water, and horizon surround the green. The hole is the most dramatic in designer Alister MacKenzie's repertoire, and probably in the world.

The sixteenth is dazzling. Every golfer dreams of playing the hole. The golfer who hasn't played it can imagine himself doing so, for the hole may be the most photographed in golfdom. I felt I knew it without playing it, in the same way that one feels one knows Augusta National without having played it; the annual Masters tournament brings Augusta National into our homes via television. My second-hand knowledge of Cypress Point, however, was nothing compared with being there.

I was years into my golfing life before I finally was invited to Cypress, as it's known, and consequently was excited when the opportunity arose. I'd been in Monterey for the opening of the new Spanish Bay links, designed by Robert Trent Jones, Jr. He was helped by Sandy Tatum, a former president of the United States Golf Association, a golf scholar, and a low-handicap player; and also by Tom Watson, who is not only one of the finest golfers, but a most thoughtful and analytical man. I played behind Watson at the course opening and later sat down to lunch with him. As always, he was direct and enlightening and the perfect person to talk to before I played Cypress. He'd played the course many times. Tatum, who was often his companion there, was a member at Cypress and had called to register me as a guest. I was told to show up early the morning after the Spanish Bay opening.

Watson played Cypress fairly often while he was a psychology student at Stanford University up the coast in Palo Alto. The sixteenth hole in particular was an ideal venue for him to test what he was learning about psychology as it applies to golf. It might also be the hole in golf that best tests one's grasp of the psychology of golf — such an important aspect of the game that some people claim golf is more a mind game than a physical game. As the saying goes, the most important distance a golfer needs to take care of is the six inches from ear to ear. This is especially true at Cypress's sixteenth, where the sea froths and the boulders along the shore seem to await one's shot like so many snapping turtles. The green seems a continent away and reachable by only the most majestic of strokes. It's all carry, and one is carrying a corner of the Pacific Ocean. To reach the green in one shot is to conquer fear. The green seems small, the ocean is vast. The hole tells you what kind of golfer you are.

I consider myself fortunate to have played Cypress and to have done so soon after my encounter with Watson. I had first visited him in December 1980, when we met in the locker room of the Kansas City Country Club, his home course in his home town. There we discussed at length the psychology of golf. We spoke frequently in the following years, and I was always sure to follow him whenever I could. He plays the game the way it should be played: without complaints, taking the breaks in stride, accepting what it brings, and always grateful for being able to spend his life doing something he enjoys.

Four years after first sitting down with Watson at his club, I again had the opportunity to engage in a lengthy, one-on-one conversation with him. This time we were seated at breakfast in the Champions' Room on the upper floor at the Augusta National Golf Club. Watson belonged here, for the room was reserved for Masters winners. He had won the 1977 Masters and had won it again in 1981. Watson had also won five British Opens and the 1982 United States Open at the Pebble Beach Golf Links, around the corner from Cypress Point. He was one of the greats of the game. He knew where he had been and where he was going. He kept his eye on the ball and he was sure of his target.

Watson has a most incisive mind. It's not only his undergraduate degree in psychology. He's thoughtful by nature, and he has a wide range of interests. He'll talk golf swing, as the saying goes, but he'll also talk politics, or environmental issues, or family life. He neither decorates himself with corporate logos on every available portion of his clothing nor tries to be anybody other than his sensible, considerate self. Watson is a reflective man whose mind reaches beyond the golf course, and it is because of his mind that I have always enjoyed chatting with him. I'd also been especially careful to watch him when he was in pressure-laden situations. Never is a champion golfer more interesting than when he has a chance to win a major championship — the Masters, United States Open, British Open, or PGA Championship. That's when I find I can best learn how golfers handle the psychological problems golf presents. I could then take what I had learned and try to apply it on the golf course. That's what I would be doing at Cypress Point.

Golf offers particularly fertile ground for examining the influence of the mind and emotion on performance. As you think, it often seems, so will you golf; and it does happen that one's state of mind will override one's swing mechanics, no matter how sound they might be. Curtis Strange has a most efficient swing, but even he can make mistakes when he isn't thinking or feeling right. Errors that begin in the mind find expression in the swing. The right frame of mind, meanwhile, can often lead to successful shots.

Watson knows this. He was playing the 1982 U.S. Open at Pebble Beach. As he approached the seventeenth green on the final day, he was tied with Jack Nicklaus, who had finished his round. Watson had hit a two-iron wide of the green on the long par-three. His ball had nestled into thick rough a few feet to the left of the green, and in a side-hill, downhill lie. Watson had to loft the ball on the green, then let it run down to the hole. He had only about fifteen feet of green to work with. Up ahead, Nicklaus thought that Watson might get the ball within ten feet of the hole, at best. Par would be a good score, bogey more likely.

Having surveyed the shot, Watson readied himself to play. "Get it close," his long-time caddie Bruce Edwards encouraged him. "Get it close, hell," Watson said. "I'm going to sink it." Then he did just that and went on to win his first U.S. Open.

Watson had it all at that moment. He was able to concentrate on the shot at hand, and he was able to still his mind and visualize the ball rolling into the hole, despite the intervening rough and the slope of the green. Feeling no anxiety, he was able to play the shot. Rather than self-destruct, as Jack Nicklaus feels many golfers do when facing important shots, Watson simply visualized the shot he wanted to execute, then let himself play it. His talent came through when he most needed it. Everything came together. The mind-body dualism to which we refer when we take ourselves apart — like a car — didn't exist for Watson during this pure moment.

Watson had for that instant overcome difficulties that make golf a most psychological game. The stationary ball and the time it takes to play the game are hardly conducive to playing instinctively or automatically. Golf brings into play what Dr. Louis Robinson in his 1897 article "The Psychology of Golf" refers to as "semi-automatic acts." The nature of the game compels us to play it consciously, with our wills, while we would prefer to play it unconsciously, with our reflexes. It is a game of attention in which there is little to stimulate our attention, but plenty to distract it: hazards such as water or sand; memories of shots gone wrong; worries about the swing. We play golf self-consciously for the most part, but ideally we would like to play it without self-consciousness.

The stationary ball causes much of our self-consciousness. There it sits at our feet, waiting to be struck. By its resting position it's asking us to hit it, taunting, teasing, suggesting that we rule its flight. And it can wait forever. Should we wait too long, our attention will waver. But should we play too quickly, we won't be ready. We might think too much. The game encourages contemplation — that's one of its charms. But it's also a source of that commonplace disease, "paralysis by analysis."

Bernard Darwin addressed this problem in 1925 in an article entitled "To Think or Not to Think: Speculation on Just How Much Mental Activity Is Good for a Golf Shot." Darwin, the grandson of evolutionist Charles Darwin, was a fine writer and a skilled player who played for Great Britain against the United States in the 1922 Walker Cup match. He knew the game, and he also knew the problems inherent in its being so much a mind game.

"I believe most of us would be restored to golfing health all the more quickly," Darwin wrote, "if we could make for ourselves a self-denying ordinance, and refrain from thinking for the minimum of one whole round." Darwin, it appears, wanted to turn golf into a reaction sport. He wanted to make the highly conscious subconscious — not a bad way of defining the main tasks of anybody working on his mental mechanics. The trick is to do it.

I needed help in this area, for my mind was often too active on the course. I could learn from conversations with such golfers as Watson. Even Darwin knew what a perilous business it was, this trying to achieve a blank mind. He quoted Sir Walter Simpson, author of *The Art of Golf* in 1887. "Golf," Simpson says, "refuses to be preserved like dead meat in tins. It is living, human and free, ready to fly away at the least sign of an attempt to catch and cage it."

Golf's slow pace exacerbates the game's mental demands. Typically, a round of golf takes at least four hours, and most of that time is spent waiting to play. The actual swing takes up almost no time at all. Arnold Palmer's swing from takeaway to impact takes 1.36 seconds. Gary Player uses 1.60 seconds. Nicklaus is probably the most deliberate golfing champion in the history of the game, but even his swing takes but 1.96 seconds. Most golfers swing the club for a total of one and a half minutes during four hours on the course. There's plenty of time for thinking between each swing — too much time for many players.

Yet the time it takes to play golf is also one of its main challenges. The rhythms of the game seem to be those of a slow waltz, but so often the mind races ahead. Golf is agonizingly slow, so labored that it becomes a battle between reason and instinct, the conscious and subconscious, will and imagination. Hence the perplexing psychology of the game, a psychology rooted in the game's nature. We may know exactly what we want to do with the ball, and our mechanics may be in good working order, but we may still find we can't hit the ball. We too easily become a victim of our imaginations — as captured in the title of a Henry James short story, *The Beast in the Jungle*, the monster that ruins swings.

Watson handled these difficulties well. He had a philosophy of the game. "You win over the game now and then," he'd told me, "but I think that golf is the most difficult sport because of the variables involved, the different playing conditions we're faced with. We don't play in a standard ball park. Though the ball is sitting, it's not always in a good lie. And just as you can't control where a ball ends up, you also can't control many other aspects of the game. Not all the time, anyway. When you're playing well, it all seems so easy. But it's hard to get your mind back on track when things aren't going well. Just keep trying. You never know when you might pop one in the hole."

A typical problem for golfers arose for me when I was playing well at Pebble Beach. Somewhere in the middle of the back nine, I started thinking about the last hole. The 540-yard par-five curves along Carmel Bay on the left, all the way from tee to green. The last thing I wanted to do was endanger my score by driving anywhere near the water. My plan was to take the water out of play by aiming well to the right. There are out-of-bounds stakes along the right side, but it would have taken a poor shot to reach them. My strategy was to use a three-wood, play down the right side, and then follow that line into the green. That way I could take the water out of play.

As I played the fifteenth, sixteenth, and seventeenth holes, I found myself thinking about the last hole. The result was that I bogeyed sixteen and mis-hit my iron into the seventeenth; luckily, I found a good lie and made par. Another par on the final hole and I still had a chance of playing to better than my handicap at Pebble. I wish I hadn't thought so much about the final hole while playing the other holes, but that's the game. I'm still not very good at coping with the time between shots. My mind wanders.

Heading for the eighteenth tee, I was nonetheless confident in my strategy. As I stood over the ball, however, my mind's eye was drawn to the ocean. Try as I did to visualize my ball flying down the right side, I saw it hooking toward the water. My plan to think positively notwithstanding, I was overcome by the feeling that I'd hit the ball exactly where I didn't want to hit it. Without warning, I went from feeling confident about the upcoming shot to fearing it; I started thinking of where I didn't want to hit the ball rather than where I did. Unfortunately, golf courses offer an infinite number of places where we shouldn't hit the ball and only a few desirable places for each shot. Why are we drawn inexorably to the hazards rather than the fairways?

But never mind. Instead of succumbing, I stepped back from the ball to gather my thoughts. But it had no effect. I was stuck with the vision of my ball hooking into the ocean.

You know what happened. I took the club back slowly enough, exercising control where I could, but then the club took off on its own path. The error that began in my mind transmitted itself to my body and articulated itself via my downswing and the route the clubhead took through the ball. Scared I would hook the ball into the sea, I aimed further right as I set up over the ball. But I must have sensed that now I was aiming too far right, toward the out-of-bounds. A sudden swing shift occurred at the top of my motion. My body veered left, taking the club with it. I came across the ball from right to left and pulled the ball into the water.

I arrive at Cypress on a day made for golf. My companion is a young radiologist from Chicago. There's breeze enough off the water to make every shot an exercise in intelligent club selection, and there are enough dark clouds in the sky to help us enjoy the game. "Nae wind, nae rain, nae golf," the Scots like to say, and I can see that today could offer any sort of weather at Cypress. "I enjoy playing in the wind," Watson told me after his round at Spanish Bay. "Normally, if you don't hit the ball fifteen feet from the hole from 125 yards out, you've hit a terrible shot. But when you're taking a five-iron from that distance and trying to keep the ball under the wind and you knock it thirty feet from the hole, you've hit a hell of a shot. If you've hit it fifteen feet from the hole, you've hit a great shot."

The opener at Cypress is a 420-yard par-four into a valley, then up to an elevated green. It's easy for me to imagine and feel the shot — downhill tee shots are a pleasure — and so I set up to the ball and swing comfortably. My swing is long through the ball, extending toward my target. No problem, then. The ball is in the air before I know it, drawing slightly before settling down. It's out there a good 260 yards.

Walking down the fairway, I feel surprised. I realize that I didn't feel any first-tee jitters. It's a pleasant change, because even with our best intentions, our nerves get the better of us.

Watson, like all golfers, has felt the jitters on the first tee. It doesn't matter who he is, a golfer will sometimes feel anxious on the first tee. Generally that's where the crowds are biggest; as well, it's your first swing of the day. You want to get off to a good start. The longest walk in golf is from the practice tee to the first tee. The golf course is the real thing; it's a different world from the practice range, and there's no getting around it.

But how is one to handle the situation? I've observed golfers on the first tee for years, and asked them. There seems to be a consensus.

First, take a couple of deep breaths. That releases some tension. And make certain that you're focused on the target. Tension shortens the muscles, which in turn can shorten the swing. Thinking of the target, meanwhile, restores freedom to a golfer's thinking and length to his swing. As a matter of fact, it's a good idea to put your mind on the target throughout the round. It's one of the best ways to deal with anxiety. It adds purpose. You've got some-where to go. You're reaching for a destination.

This idea of target is a fascinating aspect of the mental side of the game. We golf as if the ball were the target. But it's not. The idea is to send the ball to the real target — a point in the fairway, a section of the green, the hole. The trouble, however, is that we don't look at the real target. We look at the ball, which makes it easy to forget where we're going. We need to retain in our mind's eye the image of the actual target.

I think about this as I reach my ball and imagine how Watson and his colleagues would handle any creeping tension. An image of Seve Ballesteros comes into my mind. He stands behind the ball prior to each shot and takes a full practice swing while looking at his target. Watson does something similar from the side of the ball. The idea is to stretch one's vision, from *here* — the ball — to *there* — the target. It's especially important when the target isn't obvious, as is the case for my approach shot into the elevated first green at Cypress. I can't see the bottom of the flag. The target isn't obvious, so I had better generate it.

This is good stuff, and the professionals do it well most of the time. My goal as I set up to the uphill shot into the green, then, is to think target, even if I can't see the bottom of the flagstick. It's the opposite shot to the one I just had from the tee, where everything was in front of me. Now I need to carry the ball all the way to the elevated green. I'll use some imagination and visualiza-tion to do so. Jack Nicklaus, for one, doesn't hit a shot until he's got a picture in his mind of what he wants to do. Pictures can activate the swing.

But there's a problem. The lack of a definite, observable target makes me feel slightly queasy over the ball. Still, thinking of the target does help. It takes my mind off swing mechanics. Just another swing, even if I am at Cypress. I'm locked in to my target, and I swing. The ball curves right to left just a hair, then settles twenty-five feet from the hole. Two putts, and I've got my par. Good start.

Playing on, I reach the par-five, 521-yard sixth hole. I'm in the wooded area of the course now. If Watson were on the tee here,

I'm sure he wouldn't see the woods. He'd have his target picked out — left side of the fairway to open up the green, which sits downhill in a clearing. Unaffected by fear, he'd swing away and find the area of the fairway he selected. From there he could reach the green.

I see the woods. However, I've been concentrating on the target, and so my mind is quiet, my nerves settled. I can visualize the flight of the ball into the fairway and manage to come up with a longish, fairly well-placed drive. There's a chance I can reach the green, and I'd like to give it a try. But as I think about the big swing I'll need, I'm not so sure it's the right shot. Maybe it's not the right time to be aggressive. There's plenty of trouble if I miss the shot.

There's also another point of view, one that the pros share. Holding back can work its way through your game and encourage defensive golf. It's no fun to play that way. Greg Norman wouldn't; he'd go for everything. If he misses, no problem. He can live with it.

On the other hand, you can make yourself crazy by going for something out of your reach. My rule of thumb (which I don't always follow) is that if I'm uneasy about the shot, I decide not to try it. I've learned that this is the best way for me.

Fair enough. I take the conservative route, then, laying up with a three-iron that gets me 100 yards from the green. I knock my next one within twenty feet, two-putt and walk away with another par. That's four pars and a bogey. I knew I'd feel inspired at Cypress. So far, anyway, I've managed the course and myself. That's what the psychology of golf is about. One situation at a time. One shot at a time. Patience. Play your own game even when things don't go well, and accept what happens. Play on.

Watson is a master at this — especially when things don't go well. I remember what happened to him during the 1984 British Open at the Old Course in St. Andrews, Scotland. I watched from no more than ten yards away as Watson stood beside his golf bag on the right side of the seventeenth fairway the last day. He was tied with Seve Ballesteros for the lead, and Ballesteros was teeing off just ahead on the last hole. Watson had won those five British Opens, but none at the Old Course, golf's hearth and home. He drove perfectly on the seventeenth, one of golf's most famous holes.

It's known as the Road Hole because of the hard path and ancient stone wall that run directly behind the green.

Watching Watson, I wondered if he would go for the pin that was tucked in the left rear corner of the green and protected by the disquieting Road Bunker that eats into the left front of the green. Golfers have taken four and five and more shots to extricate themselves from this deep, tiny pit. The Road Bunker's significance in a golfer's playing the hole is out of all proportion to its size. It makes the pin inaccessible to all but an almost-perfect shot, high and soft and angled correctly. The shot is never easy. An Open championship hung in the balance as Watson considered his options in the fairway.

Watson deliberated between a two- and a three-iron. In the end, he selected the two-iron. He was going to draw the ball toward the pin, looking for a chance at a birdie.

The shot went wrong from the start. It headed for the middle of the green and never drew. Instead, it faded slightly and flew into the right center of the green before bounding over and near the wall. Watson could only bounce the ball onto the green from there, nowhere near the hole. Meanwhile, Ballesteros holed a birdie putt at the last green. The crowd roared; I could see Ballesteros on the green punching the air with his right hand. He'd done what he had to do. Watson hadn't.

To watch Watson, though, was to see class. He didn't flinch, simply two-putted and walked to the last tee. That's the way he's always played the game. Hit the shot, observe the result, and walk on.

"I would hit that same shot again in the same situation," Watson told me some time later. "Everyone thinks I mis-clubbed, that I should have hit the three-iron. But I didn't have too much club. I just hit it right of where I wanted to hit it. I was on the upslope, and I had 210 yards to the hole. When you're on an upslope, hitting into the wind, you feel the ball is going to get up in the air. I figured the ball would carry about 200 yards, come down and be right there. I hit the same shot in practice rounds several times. This time it didn't work. I've got no regrets."

No regrets. I like that. It's easy in golf to get lost in the past,

to ask "What if?" But the challenge of the game is to leave the
past behind and focus on the present. The only shot I can control
is the one I have to play now. It's self-evident, but I forget it.

The eighth at Cypress Point is a jewel, a 338-yard par-four dogleg
right bordered by white sand hills at the bend. The green is well
round to the right, invisible from the tee, and framed by scrub and
sand. The ideal play from the tee is a high fade around the corner,
long enough to make sure you reach the fairway before the ball
begins to curve, and curvy enough so that you don't go through
the fairway. The hole sets up for a fade.

On the tee, though, I'm in a quandary. I'm having trouble picking my target; not because I can't see the portion of the fairway
upon which I want to land my ball — I can create that image in
my mind — but because I've been hitting the ball right to left all
day, not left to right. My wires are crossed; I know that the fade
is the proper shot, but I'm not confident I can hit it. It's as if the
past few holes must dictate my play on this hole. I've got too much
time to think. I need some of that Watsonian philosophy, but he's
not with me at Cypress. Still, the conversation we had yesterday
is current in my mind. It's easy to think of what he might say.

Watson would know how I'm feeling. I've seen him when he's
confident and when he's not. There are times a player feels secure
about a certain flight of the ball, and he'd like to continue using
it. At the same time, he knows it isn't the right shot. The hole doesn't
set up for it. There's a proper shot to play, one that conforms to
the shape of the hole, but he's nervous about trying it. Something
is telling him to stick with what he's doing. And the nervousness
comes from knowing — subconsciously — that he's about to choose
the wrong shot. He's going against the grain of the course.

The thing to recognize, Watson might say, is that the situation
I'm in presents one of golf's intriguing psychological dilemmas. Do
I go ahead and trust the first image that comes into my mind, or
do I revert to form? Do I play in the spirit of the game, accepting
what the course challenges me to do, or do I try to pummel the
course into my own image? To me, golf is challenging because every
shot is different. If I don't accept this, I'll put pressure on myself.

Watson would know what to do. I think he would step away from the ball for a second and try to work himself into the configuration of the hole. He'd want to feel part of the hole and sense his swing shaping itself to the way the hole moves. That's one good way to overcome the psychological inhibition a golfer might feel when he's forcing a shot against the landscape. The idea is to turn the mental into the physical.

The objective was clear. I could best feel the swing by putting myself into the frame of the hole. I was anxious because I had disconnected from the shape of the hole. Now I wanted to re-establish that connection in a natural way.

The fade it was, then. I aimed twenty yards left of the turn and then slid my ball around. The strategy of becoming part of the course had proven an innovative way to deal with anxiety. Fit yourself to the configuration of the hole. If harmony is the goal, harmonize, an approach that promotes relaxation. It helps produce the state of being mentally engaged and physically relaxed — an attractive way to play the game.

Course management is an important part of this strategy. Watson once decided to try and drive the green on the par-four, 291-yard ninth hole at Cypress during a practice round. The green is thumbnail size and sits on a hill surrounded by sand and rough ground. He went for it anyway and made the green. "Will you do that in the tournament?" his playing companions asked. "Sure," Watson answered, "if I want to make seven every day." Watson knew the difference between practice and play. He could manage himself.

I tried to do the same. The round went along smoothly, at least until I reached the fourteenth hole. I had hit a few putts up to that point that weren't stroked confidently. But they also weren't bad putts; the longer ones ran up within a foot or two, and the shorter putts bounced uneasily rather than rolling into the hole with authority. I wasn't hitting the ball solidly on the greens.

Again, I thought of Watson. Golf is an inward enough game, so why not imagine I'm somebody else? I like doing this while on the course because it's a good way to get out of myself. It's what was once called the "as if" philosophy. Pretend you're somebody else; imagine you're swinging like somebody else. I have often modeled my putting stroke after Watson's, because nobody putted better than he did for years. His putter blade came through the ball so squarely and so assuredly. The ball came off as if it were on a track and invariably caught the middle of the hole, with speed. Every time Watson stepped over a putt from about 1974 to 1984, it looked as if he were going to make it.

But this was 1987, and Watson was in his sixteenth year on the pro tour. His short game and putting had seemed impaired by some defect, a weak link. Nowadays when he stood over a short putt, it wasn't a sure thing at all. He would later miss a three-foot putt to lose the 1988 World Series of Golf to Mike Reid. The putt was weak. It never looked in.

Such putts were easy for Watson not that long ago. But now, having missed some crucial putts, he wasn't confident. People told him to remember the good times when he was putting well, and to call upon those feelings now, to think positively. Watson would have liked to think positively. "But I can't convince myself that I'm going to hit a solid putt when I've been missing putts," he said. "Confidence comes from good strokes, from seeing the ball go in the hole. I haven't done that for a while."

I wonder. Sports psychologists believe that we can create successful golf shots by programming our minds properly. The proposition that factors other than mass and velocity influence the flight of the golf ball is extraordinary. When I'm playing well, I am also seeing the target well, much as a baseball batter says he is seeing the ball clearly when he's hitting well. But can the golfer compel himself to think positively? What comes first, the positive thoughts or the good swings that bring successful results? Maybe Watson should project a more confident self — even if it is the self he was then, not now. Can't he pretend he's a terrific putter, and then putt as if he is?

That's a good idea, but Watson isn't one to fool himself. Maybe he's studied too much psychology, or maybe he's too much of a realist. I think he's just being sensible. How can you convince yourself you're putting well when you're not? I tense up even more when I try to do that. It makes more sense for me to accept what's going on, and then do the best I can. That helps me relax. I'm not fooling myself. I'd like to, but I can't.

How does a golfer hit the shot, then, or go after a putt, when he's not confident, or when he's not concentrating?

Golfers who understand the psychology of the game, and of themselves, revert to instinct. A player will be nervous a lot of times in golf. The feeling will come and go, and many times you won't know why it came or why it left. It's as if we've all got an endless variety of impulses that show up when they want to, not when we want them to. I've never been able to figure out, for instance, why I can go to the golf course feeling good, get out on the range, and then find that the club feels as heavy as a shovel; on other days, it's as light as a feather. I can't develop a touch either way. The clubhead is a weight, or else I can hardly feel it in my hands. How am I supposed to play?

In one way, I don't think I can do much about the situation. That is, I can't easily change the way I'm responding. I can try to visualize a good shot, but if I can't do that, I've still got to hit the shot. I can also try to calm myself down. But I try not to worry when I can't. There's no evidence that a golfer can't hit great shots when he's nervous. A golfer's stroke and swing don't disappear. They're his. They'll be there whether he likes it or not. Again, I advise thinking of the target. That encourages rhythm and tempo. Get your rhythm and tempo under control and you can make your best swing. You get away from your mind that way. Although there is a lot of psychology in golf, the idea is to get to the point where there's very little. You do that by turning the game into a reaction sport. You'll increase your anxiety if you think of the parts of your swing at such a time, or if you force what you think are the correct thoughts. The more productive strategy is to connect yourself to the target and swing.

Watson was nervous when he faced a four-footer on the last green to win the 1975 British Open at Carnoustie. "It was the most important putt of my life because it could make me a champion," he told writer Michael McDonnell. "My legs were weak. I couldn't think straight."

What was Watson supposed to do to calm down? Should he have

gone to the side of the green and done a few yoga exercises, meditated for a minute or two? Forget it. His mind was in disarray. He simply stepped up to the putt and hit it. And he holed it.

"That was instinct," Watson said. "There was no point in thinking about it."

What was Watson saying here? I think he meant that a golfer can't be a Buddhist. He must live in the world. That world includes a series of problems on the course. Every shot is different, and it's possible that every situation will elicit feelings over which he has little control. Experience will help a golfer calm down, but anxiety can always show up in such a slow game. Nicklaus teed it up on the first hole of the 1987 Masters, a year after his dramatic win at age forty-six. He was so nervous on that opening tee that he hit what he later called the worst drive of his life on that particular hole. There was little he could do on demand to settle his nerves. That's human nature. Nicklaus is often thought to concentrate better than any golfer who ever played. At the same time, though, he gets nervous, and he can't always control his reaction.

"Some tension gets into me," Nicklaus once told me as I watched him practice in Florida. "Tension has always been a problem for me. It usually shows up in my right arm; it stiffens up. It's been that way for years."

Nicklaus first noticed the stiffness during the 1964 Masters. He was on the twelfth tee in the last round, and Masters co-founders Clifford Roberts and Bobby Jones were off to his right.

"I noticed them," Nicklaus said, "and I could feel the tension come into my right arm. It went dead stiff. I shanked the ball short of the water. It's something that I handle well sometimes, but other times I don't."

Watson, like all golfers, has had similar feelings. He may decide to hit a short putt firmly, but the decision doesn't always register with his arms and hands. He hits the ball weakly, decelerating through the ball, and comes up a couple of inches short. With the best will in the world, and thinking of the target, he misses the putt. His nervous system won't obey his command. That's what happens to me on the fourteenth at Cypress. I hit a thirty-foot putt six feet past the hole as I lose all sense of arm speed through the ball. Then

I take too long a backstroke and cut my stroke off at the ball, which hobbles to a halt a foot short of the hole.

It doesn't matter, though. I've got the fifteenth and the sixteenth holes to look forward to. They're back-to-back par-threes, and the fifteenth, though little known because of its neighbor, the famous sixteenth, is one of the finest short holes in the world. It's just 139 yards across the surf and rocks to a green behind which is a wild tangle of gnarled old cypress trees. The hole is a beauty; I could hit nine-irons into the green all day. This day, meanwhile, I hit a punched nine-iron, keeping the ball under the wind. It pulls up fifteen feet from the hole, and I take two putts for my par. On to the sixteenth.

I've looked forward all day to the tee ball at the sixteenth, and now I want to hit the green. That would mean a successful day; to hit the sixteenth at Cypress is to be a golfer.

There's little choice but to hit the driver. The wind is slightly into me and left to right. I'll aim for the left side of the green and let the wind take the ball in. Standing over the ball, though, all I can see is the ball heading for the ocean.

"Take it easy," I tell myself, as I try to get into the shot. I remind myself that this might be the most exciting shot in the game and that the world's greatest players miss the green regularly. My nervousness is expected, but it is more than a little unsettling. I can't hit the shot feeling so uneasy.

Watson goes back to basics at times like this. He sets his feet properly while going through his check list of fundamentals. This is a sensible strategy. Nervousness is one thing, the racing mind is one thing, but proper mechanics are another. I'll make a serious mental error if I don't put myself into a decent position from which to swing. I call this a mental error because it derives from a fault in thinking, or inattention. After all, setting my feet properly is something I can control. I haven't started to take the club back yet, which is when the subconscious kicks in. Maybe I can't do a thing once I take the club back, but I can control the static aspects of the game, such as setup. There's no excuse for an error at that stage. Watson made sure he set up properly to that putt at Carnoustie, didn't he? Surely I can incorporate the same presence of mind.

The first step is just that, a step — away from the ball. I've been racing. Now's the time to try to slow down. People get too fast in their thoughts; their swing follows. The trick is to walk more slowly, to breathe slowly, keep my thoughts slow. Swing the club-head more slowly. These things aren't always easy to do, but at least I can prepare myself for the shot. I want to give myself a decent chance. The game is tough enough. Why make it harder?

The self-talk takes effect. After removing myself from the problems of the shot, I become enchanted by the splendor of the environment. Spellbound for a moment, I feel quiet and set up to the ball smartly. My mind's eye is fixed firmly on the target. I swing the driver, and the ball takes off toward the left side of the green, coming down just a few feet short. I'm feeling good. My chip finishes five feet from the hole, but I miss the putt. Still, I played the hole well. That memory will travel. I play seventeen and eighteen, enjoying the late morning, falling in line with the lilt of the game while accepting that I can't understand perfectly the machinery of the mind. Golf is a means of learning about ourselves. To address the game's psychology is to appreciate that the best way to deal with it is to come up with a philosophy. There are no answers, but what's the matter with searching over eighteen holes for ideas?

After playing Cypress, I pack my clubs up in the car and then drive along the coast before stopping to sit on an outcropping of rock. Out comes my notebook.

The psychology of golf can be as complex as we let it. But it can also be simple if we just allow for human nature. Chatting with Watson and following him over the years have helped me immeasurably. He and his fellow pros deal with the same mysteries as the amateur golfer. We're all beginners when it comes to understanding the mind. The game, and human nature, are bigger than our ability to comprehend every nuance.

I've made a beginning. Having read so much on the psychology of the game since my years at university, I thought I had to have complete understanding of the nuances if I were going to play well. But this understanding is elusive; besides, the search for answers adds flavor to the game and makes us the richer for playing it. It's pleasant to tussle with the questions, even if we can't figure out all the answers.

The study of golf psychology braces the mind. It's neither a black art nor an exact science. Concentration; attention; human will; judgment; perception; the conscious, subconscious, and unconscious determinants of performance; imagination and intelligence; instinct and reason; neurology; the roles of the autonomic and central nervous systems: Such are the elements that comprise this side of the game. But I can hardly expect to play very well while examining each in detail as I stand over a shot.

I can, however, remember Cypress and the lessons I have learned from Watson. I can accept the complexities of the game and the intricacies of the human being. Neither one is simple. This approach may generate a sense of humor as I work toward better golf, for the golfer who can't laugh at the perfect tee shot that lands in a divot has no chance.

It's also important to take stock. How far do I want to go in golf? How much work am I willing to put in? Maybe I should be happy for the few good shots a round, and forget the many lesser efforts. It's human nature to grumble after a round. Or is it?

I've learned from Watson that I should examine my personality. Am I high-strung or easygoing? Am I aggressive by nature or more reserved? Am I competitive, or does score matter very little? And how do I react to stress? Golfers tend to revert to their essential natures when under pressure. So why not examine that nature and let it guide me on the course?

The beauty of golf's psychology is that it brings us into contact with ourselves — truth in the shape of arcs, planes, and flights of golf balls, instant readouts. The result doesn't matter that much in the long run. Golf's a game. It enables us to spend four or five hours alone with our thoughts, feelings, and wishes. The traffic on the course is mostly the commotion in our own minds. To think of one solution is to come up with a thesaurus of alternatives. That's why it's so satisfying when we manage to lance the congestion for a while, when we break through to the free swing. The idea is to balance the complexities of the game and our own natures. That's a route to coping with the game's psychology.

I like to let golf be a means of expression, a creative act. Every shot is an opportunity. Hit it and forget it. Then hit it again and forget it. That's when the game will be the most gratifying. And when it's enjoyable, I'll be relaxed. That's the best way to play the game.

# In the Zone

The eleventh hole at the Ballybunion Golf Club in County Kerry, Ireland, is breathtaking. The tee of the 443-yard par-four on this wild, roaming course hard by the Atlantic Ocean sits high above a three-tiered fairway. Standing there one fall day, while playing in a confection known as the World Writers Cup, I felt almost too absorbed by my surroundings. The lay of the land was such that I could see all the way down the fairway, up and down and along the sea, into a narrow opening bordered by sand dunes, then the green. The opening to the green was a sort of passageway, a secret world available only to the finest of shots. Beyond, meanwhile, was primitive golfing land, dunes everywhere, and the sea as backdrop. Captivated, I nearly forgot that I had a shot to play. I wanted to hit the fairway, and to hit it just so, without a trace of push. The ocean was a glorious sight, but with the wind blowing left to right, I didn't want to fade the ball at all. If that happened — and the fade was my customary shot — I'd be hitting three from the tee.

That I didn't need, since I was one hole down to my opponent with eight to play.

I couldn't settle down; there was too much *view*. I needed to switch my focus so that my attention would be in the right place — on the shot. Or at least I thought I did.

Then something happened that I have on reflection found illuminating. Peter Dobereiner, the seasoned golf correspondent from the *Observer* in London, descended to the tee from a promontory upon which he had perched himself as non-playing captain of the British side. For all the agitation his sudden presence had aroused in me, he might as well have been Bobby Jones or Jack Nicklaus. Dobers, as his colleagues know him, had met and known every golfer of the last few decades, from Ben Hogan to Seve Ballesteros, and he knew them well. He was also sensitive to the effects of the mind on performance in golf, ever sympathetic to human frailty, sometimes even expecting it, and all too aware of how the swing could come apart.

As I planted my feet self-consciously, I grew hypersensitive to Dobereiner's hulking figure behind me, not to mention the ocean to my right and the rugged terrain left of the fairway. Foolish as I knew the feeling was, I wanted to show Dobereiner, and myself, that I could hit a good shot when under strain. I thought he cared what I did. The truth is that nobody cares how you hit a shot; as the story goes on the professional tours, when a golfer comes into the locker room and describes the quadruple-bogey eight he made on the sixth hole, his colleagues are saying to themselves, "Who cares? I wish it would have been a nine."

Instead of focusing my attention on hitting a good shot, I was trying *not* to hit a bad shot; that's a small difference in words here, but a big difference in practice. The former attitude breeds tension, the Number One swing-wrecker.

The feeling lasted only a moment. While over the ball, I laughed silently. "Peter doesn't give a damn what you do," I told myself. "And if you hit your shot onto the beach, so what? You've hit ridiculous shots before and you'll hit them again. So just pick your target and swing."

The internal chat calmed me. I visualized my swing flowing

through the ball toward my target and the ball soaring down the middle of the fairway. Why did I feel so calm, when I had been so anxious just a moment before? It was as if I had released a pressure valve. The anxiety seemed to float out of me into the Irish sky. Then I swung, effortlessly, smoothly. The ball followed the exact flight path I had envisaged. Dobereiner said, "Fine shot," and moved on.

From then on, I was a different golfer. My pace picked up as I approached each shot with curiosity and excitement. It was just me, the golf ball, and my target. I sent my second shot through the slot into the eleventh green. It finished near the hole, and I made the birdie putt. Then came birdies on the twelfth, thirteenth, and sixteenth, as I went on to win the match. I had gone from one down to three up.

Looking back, I remember a clarity of purpose prior to hitting the ball during that series of glittering holes. I could see the ball flying to my target. My feeling over the ball was of poise and balance; I felt light on my feet at the same time that I felt ready to go; it was as if I were in a runner's starting position. My swing was all of a piece — continuous, segments smoothly joined and unified — while through the ball I felt carried along, swept away to a balanced finish position. Movement analysts have a phrase for the space a dancer occupies and within which he or she moves; it's known as a kinesphere. Its outer dimensions are formed by how far the dancer can extend while maintaining balance. At best, there is maximum extension and arc, governed by stability within a dynamic form. That's how I felt at Ballybunion — athletic, energetic, extended, under control.

This was the golf of which I dreamt I was capable but had known so rarely. I wanted more of it, more of what I have come to call my "Ballybunion feeling." It's a feeling that philosopher-psychologist William James described. "An athlete sometimes wakens suddenly to an understanding of the fine points of the game and to a real enjoyment of it. . . . If he keeps on engaging in the sport, there may come a day when all at once the game plays itself through him — when he loses himself in some great contest."

This is the most satisfying way of playing golf, but it happens infrequently. I seem to play my way into it by accident rather than being able to call upon it. That's what I'd like to do, as would all golfers, especially touring professionals who depend on the game for their living. But they don't know how to produce the state either. They get into it more often than amateurs, but it descends upon them or, better, overtakes them. It's a dreamy experience, eerie to watch and fascinating to hear described.

I traveled to Las Vegas in the winter of 1983 to seek out Johnny Miller, the golfer who in 1974 and 1975 touched the highest peaks of the game. He won eight tournaments in 1974, then the 1975 Tucson and Phoenix Opens back-to-back, shooting twenty-four under par and twenty-five under par respectively. His play was uncanny. Time after time he hit shots the exact distance to the flagstick. His play then tapered off, and he rarely played that kind of golf again. The zone he inhabited in the mid-1970s is a foreign country that he later visited for a few shots at a time, perhaps a round here and there. He wanted the experience again, but it's elusive. Tom Watson puts it this way: "You can get close enough to mastering the game to feel it, to breathe it maybe, to smell it. But you can't master it, not for a long time. Ben Hogan may be the only person to have really come close to it for a long time. And also Byron Nelson. He came awfully close to hitting the ball the way it should be struck, and also with the scoring part of the game." Hogan is still acknowledged as the one man who could control the flight of the ball shot after shot. Nelson won eleven tournaments in a row in 1945; his swing was powerful and elegant and always on track.

Miller was the same those few years ago. Now, seated in a plush, purple lounge chair in a hotel room high above Las Vegas, Miller recalls his play. To hear him speak, one might think he's talking about a person other than himself.

"I had it all then," Miller tells me. "I hit the ball well with the long clubs, was great with my irons, and putted excellently. I was into something I guess few players have known, maybe none in my era. It was sort of the golfing nirvana, and it had nothing to do with the mental side of the game. It was totally physical. I'd go out on the practice tee in early 1975, hit twenty-five or thirty balls and say, 'Perfect, why am I here?' I'd say my average iron shot for three months in 1975 was within five feet of my line. I was hitting an average of sixteen greens a round. Guys win hitting thirteen greens a round.''

What might account for such precision? Miller answered quickly.

"I had such great eyesight and depth perception. I knew what 147 yards was. I knew exactly the difference between 147 yards and 149 yards, and I could feel it. A lot of people hit the ball on line, but don't get the right distance. I did it by taking every club back the same distance, to the same position in my backswing. It didn't matter if I was hitting a half shot or a full shot. The club went back to the same place, and then my whole thing was varying clubhead speed. That's all I was doing. I would take a five-iron back and say, 'Okay, this is going to be 100 miles per hour, or 95, or 90.' Most guys try to vary distance by choking down on the club, gripping it lighter, swinging softer or harder, or taking a bigger or smaller shoulder turn. But these things had nothing to do with my swing. It was like a pitcher who would make the same windup and then change only the speed of his delivery. That's what I was doing. I was taking the identical windup with each shot, and even the same follow-through, but just changing the speed at the bottom of my swing.''

Miller's play affected golfers in his group. They were befuddled. But what could they do? He didn't know how he came upon this so-called nirvana, nor could he have advised them where they might find it. Yet he didn't seem to be doing anything much different from what they were. It was just that his swings were more refined, that the ball off the clubface sounded sweeter, that his shots finished closer to the hole. The atmosphere around him was quiet, as if reflecting the simplicity in his mind. To be near him was to feel serene, privy to some magical experience that defined what one could achieve in golf.

"I had more guys blowing shots over the greens,'' Miller continued. "It got quite bad in my prime. I was taking this big long swing and hitting the ball nowhere, just concerning myself with accuracy. I'd hit a five-iron because that was the shot I wanted to hit, a real soft shot. Or I'd use a six-iron into a green that was soft and tilted back to front, take a big swing — although it was way too much club — and hit the ball with no spin whatsoever. It would just knuckle up there, hit the green and go pfft, just staying there. The guys hitting after me would see I'd hit a six-iron with this big swing and say no way, it couldn't be more than a seven. They'd hit the seven and blow it right over the green, or they'd hit a shot with so much spin it would suck back twenty-five feet. I had to tell the guys not to look in my bag to see what I'd hit. After I hit the shot I'd tell my caddie I hit it real soft, just to help them, because I knew they were listening."

Miller carried himself back easily to his best days, speaking without any hesitation. He was talking, I thought, as he once golfed: with complete freedom and direct contact established between his thoughts, feelings, expressions, and his words. How odd that he could not find this mood with a golf club in his hands now, when it was with a golf club in his hands that the mood was previously generated.

Miller controlled his swing in those days. This was not a control born of willfulness, but entirely the opposite. The golfing muse had descended upon him; he was the favored recipient and talented enough to let it find full expression. He felt connected, via the shaft of the club, to the clubhead, and through the contact he could conjure so readily. From the clubhead to the ball, his body would unwind on the throughswing, as he felt completely in touch with his target. In some way, the club swung him. Miller went along for the ride. It was as if he could stretch himself out all along the fairway and touch the pin. Every golf swing felt slow to him; he felt that he had so much time to complete his swing. A new game — the game we all seek — burst through his normal patterns, and he played by sensation, and sensation alone. No wonder he talks about it now with a sense of amazement.

"It was that I had the means of controlling distance," he tells me. "I could feel the shot so well. That gave me more shot options, more arrows in my quiver. Most golfers, say, hit a five-iron 175 yards with their normal swing. If they go right to left with the draw, they'll hit it 180; if they play left to right with the fade, they'll hit it 170. That gives them a ten-yard variance with full swings. That's a good way to vary distance. But the trouble in golf so often is that if the pin is left and you're between clubs, you really don't want to hit the ball left to right, so now what do you do? The draw shot will go too far. I could do more things because I was down to a two-yard variance with clubs, since I could vary clubhead speed. It was as if I could hit more notes on the scale. And I think that's the ultimate way of controlling distance, to have a set way of taking the club back, then applying the different speeds. It's like shooting a basketball. You set it the same way for a short shot as for a long shot, but you just don't put as much effort into it."

Miller's memories continue to tumble forth. He stands up to emphasize a point, then swings his arms round as if he were making a swing. Years have passed since he and the game were so synchronized with one another, but something is coming alive in him now, a deep-seated memory of golfing perfection.

Johnny Miller isn't the only golfer to have played this way, although he enjoyed the adventure longer than most. Jack Nicklaus was in the groove in 1980 when he won the U.S. Open at Baltusrol Golf Club in New Jersey. As often happens, he was most aware of releasing stored-up energy through the ball. He was holding on; the club was propelling him forward.

"It was through the ball," Nicklaus says, recalling the sensation that came and went like a summer storm. "I felt the toe of the club coming up in the air and flying through to a finish, from a perfect backswing position. I felt that during the last nine holes at Baltusrol. I was absolutely killing it straight."

Tom Watson has also felt it. I recall his two-iron shot to the last green during the 1983 British Open at Royal Birkdale. He needed to par the hole to win, and as the crowds gathered around him, sensing his fifth Open championship, I wondered how a golfer's mind can be quiet at a time like this. One swing for the Open, and plenty of opportunity to out-think oneself, for anxiety to dispel the calmness. Not, however, if the golfer is locked in. And Watson was locked in.

I'll never forget it. Watson stood beside his ball and asked his caddie Alfie Files, "How far have we got?" "Two-thirteen to the hole," Files responded. Without hesitation, Watson took his two-iron, set up, and swung. The ball headed directly for the flag, but Watson could not see its flight. The crowd surged ahead of him as soon as he contacted the ball. None of this mattered. Watson knew he had hit the shot he needed. "That's it," he said to Files, "as good as I can do." The ball settled fifteen feet short of the hole, right on line. Watson was somewhere in the massed crowd in the fairway. He emerged accompanied by a policeman. Raising his arms in triumph, he walked onto the green, two-putted, and won the Open. I remember those few moments as a singular example of concentration. Watson was in a different world, and he rose to the occasion required by the different world on the last hole of an Open championship.

"It was exactly the type of shot I planned," Watson would say later. "I was in a left-to-right wind, and I was going to draw it slightly into the wind. It was right on the flag all the way, and though I never saw it land because there were so many people, I knew when it came down it was splitting the flag, not right or left, but right on it."

Watson had discovered, for that ultimate shot, and for much of that British Open, that golf can absorb every faculty. He hit the perfect shot. "Ideally," he once said, "the ball should be struck with an accelerated motion in the middle of the clubface with the clubhead moving along the chosen line, not inside or outside the line." For golfers of Watson's caliber, it sometimes takes a championship the magnitude of a British Open to jolt them out of their habitual, analytical ways. This isn't to say the Ballybunion feeling arrives on demand in a major; not at all, or else Watson and his elite brethren would be scoring nothing at courses that require everything in the way of shot-making. Nirvana rarely arrives on schedule. Winners invariably find it, or it finds them. But rarely does it happen on demand.

Take Bruce Lietzke. He was in golf's dreamworld in 1977 during a period of a few weeks in which he won two tournaments and shot par or better in twenty-two rounds. Years later he looked upon his experiences with wonder, not only for what he felt, but for how quickly he found himself back in the real world of worried thoughts and missed shots.

"It was not a real strong feeling of being invincible," Lietzke told me, "but I had no fear of any golf shot, no fear of any putt, no fear of pressure. They were weeks in which the mental and the physical were together, though again, not as intense as Watson and Nicklaus have had it. I would go back to my room after one of those rounds where everything jelled. I'd think about it and I'd realize I couldn't remember hearing yardages from my caddie. I know I did hear them because it's important for my club selection. It was a free-flowing time. I'd hear a yardage and I'd grab a club. No negative thoughts. I'd set up, usually playing very fast, no waggling of the club. I was ready to pull the trigger and hit. I'll have one of those rounds and I'll go back to my room and might not remember who I played with. You're so into it that you block out a lot of other things outside you."

Greg Norman, the outstanding Australian golfer, gets into the groove quite often. I've seen him shoot some remarkable rounds of golf, a sixty-four the final round of the 1988 Masters after starting the day eleven shots from the lead, a record-setting sixty-five in the first round of the 1986 PGA Championship at the Inverness Club in Toledo, Ohio. These rounds were special — both for him to play and for me to watch. The late psychologist Abraham Maslow would have called them peak experiences. Norman was able to do exactly what he wanted with the golf ball. He toyed with the courses. There was something otherworldly about watching him, he was that self-possessed.

I think especially of the sixty-five Norman shot at Inverness. Serious as the round was — this was, after all, a major championship — Norman was loose. He joked with his playing partners Hubert Green and Larry Nelson. He waved to his three-year-old daughter Morgan-Leigh as she followed him in a stroller. And when he got to his ball, he relished the shot.

Norman demonstrated just how exalted a state a golfer could get in when he played the eighteenth hole. He had 120 yards to the pin, which was tucked into the front left corner of the small green that sits behind shaggy rough and bunkers. More important, he had 128 yards to the top ridge of the green, where he wanted his ball to land.

"I aim the ball according to how I want it to finish," Norman would say after his round. At the eighteenth, he decided to hit his nine-iron twenty-five feet to the right of the hole and twenty feet beyond it, allowing the ball to spin back and to the left. He swung and the ball danced around the green.

Fred Astaire couldn't have tiptoed around the flag more adroitly than did Norman's ball. It hit the green exactly where he wanted, swung left ninety degrees, took the slope, and reversed itself toward the hole, finishing ten feet away. It was a command performance.

"When you're playing well," Norman said, "you can hit the ball within a foot of where you want it to land."

I felt a similar sense of control when I shot seventy-three at Sunningdale's Old Course, near London. Only the day before I had played indifferent golf at Coombe Hill. It was a rush getting to Coombe Hill, and then my companion and I had to hurry off the first tee. But all was peaceful at Sunningdale. Traffic had been light, the morning was gentle, and I was visiting another hallowed home of golf. I was so in tune with the environment that I felt I would play well, and play well I did. There wasn't a shot I didn't feel comfortable with. I was involved, each shot a challenge rather than a concern. Isn't this one of the reasons we play golf? Each of us has hit shots to remember, shots that occurred when the game was simple.

Strange things happen at these times. A golfer who has returned from the exalted state looks back and recalls an incident that he is convinced led to his entry into his altered world. One feels destiny played a part. Bobby Jones was convinced that destiny takes hold, particularly in majors. We all have our majors, though; we can all anticipate being taken over just at the appropriate moment. And then we can really play golf. Jones did it for much of his career, but especially in his Grand Slam year of 1930, when he won the U.S. and British Amateurs and Opens. Nick Faldo has also done it, most emphatically during the 1989 Masters, and all, he said, because of a series of circumstances that conspired to arouse him enough to enter the magical zone.

Early in the week of that Masters, a newsman had said Faldo wasn't a capable enough putter to win majors, which were generally played on courses with extremely fast putting greens. He had won the 1987 British Open at Muirfield in Scotland, but that was with his trademark meticulous driving and iron play. His putting at the 1989 Masters was adequate, but not inspired; at least it wasn't until after he read the writer's disparaging comments.

Prior to the final round of the Masters, Faldo changed putters. He worked with his new putter during two twenty-minute sessions before teeing off, and then, as if it were destined, he holed a fifty-one-foot putt to birdie the opening hole. This was not the sort of putt a golfer expects to make. Two putts for par would have been acceptable.

That monster first putt was only the beginning. Faldo's putter turned into a magic wand as he holed putt after putt across Augusta National's speedy greens, which have contours reminiscent of warped record albums. When he came to the sixteenth hole, Faldo holed what he called "just a joke" of a putt, straight downhill with eight feet of break. Destiny had touched him. He had found the not-often-found, and on the second play-off hole, the course's eleventh, he sunk a thirty-foot birdie putt in near darkness to defeat Scott Hoch and win the Masters.

"Yeah, you do believe that fate plays a part," Faldo said later. "I've seen it happen to others. I've watched Nicklaus shoot sixty-five to win the Masters. . . . For me to hole ridiculous putts, and to be given one opportunity to win it, and to do it, it amazes me."

But maybe we can do something to help fate along. Since we seem to play our best when we're loose, why not loosen things up by taking an off-kilter approach to a round? Golf is a game, a recreation. It's meant to be fun, so let's play at it. Let's encourage our creative sides.

Most of us take the game seriously. We work hard over shots, grip the club so tensely we can't possibly have any feeling in our forearms and hands. How big is that golf ball anyway? How heavy? Why do we think we have to apply such force? Ballesteros agrees that setup is important, but he also points out that because golf is played on land of varying topography, every shot is different.

The idea is to feel comfortable. Bobby Jones said that golf can't be played with tension. Now when I play I don't care as much about exact vectors, angles, and lines when I set up. I'm careful, having learned the importance of setup, but I'm not a stickler for perfect form. I feel differently each day; my metabolism is different. Consequently, I feel differently over the ball. Work on setup on the range, get the general principles down, and then work easily into position on the course. Your muscles will have a better chance to relax. The Ballybunion feeling will have a better chance to show itself.

Do anything to make the game pleasant. That's what I'm learning. Gary Player checks out the flowers and trees that border some holes, thereby freeing his mind from worries about the game. "Hmmm," he says to himself, "I wonder where that flower came from, what kind it is." PGA Tour pro Dave Barr won't even approach his shot until it's time to play. He prefers to walk around or hold back. There's a time and a place for everything. Don't make the shot so important that it occupies all your thinking. Savor the surroundings.

Even superstitions can help. Curtis Strange has taken to wearing a red shirt when he's in contention heading into the final round of a major championship; he won his first U.S. Open that way, and then he won the 1989 U.S. Open, his second, wearing a red shirt. If it feels good, do it. Seve Ballesteros often listens to positive-thinking tapes in the evening prior to an important round. Payne Stewart was into acupuncture for a while; he was convinced that applying pressure to certain points around his ears helped him play well. Irishman Dave Feherty listens to opera and Woody Allen tapes before playing. LPGA golfer Colleen Walker convinced herself that she could trigger images of a successful performance by touching a spot just below her navel — there's no scientific basis to this, but she believed it worked for her. Who's to argue? Walker played very well in the late 1980s while doing so. Ray Floyd, meanwhile, plants what he describes as bizarre images in his mind's eye to help him transport himself into a trance. "You'd think I'm crazy if I told you some of the things I come up with," he says. Well, at least he's doing something internal; we golfers so often look outside ourselves for help. Instead, we should get into ourselves; golf *is* an individual game that offers many possibilities for self-exploration. A golf course consists of 150 acres for exploration. Ballesteros is one of the best golfers at getting himself locked in. He says that he gets into a bubble of concentration. I'd drive hundreds of miles to see him, because something spectacular is sure to happen. He's excitable; his facial expressions, head moves, and body twists make his golf physical; maybe that's why his swing is so free and fluid. He's rambunctious and will try anything.

I watched him during the 1987 Ryder Cup matches at the Muirfield Village Golf Club in Dublin, Ohio. What a show he put on. During one foursomes competition, or alternate shots as it's known in America, Ballesteros and his partner José-Maria Olazabal were tied after fourteen holes with Payne Stewart and Larry Nelson. Olazabal had put Ballesteros into an awkward position in heavy rough on a hill beside the fifteenth green. Big deal; Ballesteros, golf's Houdini, relished the challenge. He popped the ball out of the rough and onto the crest of a hump — one specific hump — and watched as the ball slid down near the hole. Ballesteros and Olazabal won the hole and went on to win the match.

Ballesteros plays golf the way it should be played. He savors it. He's more fun to watch when he's missing fairways and short putts than other golfers are when they're hitting and making them. He turns a golf course into a theater. He's a performer. I think that's how we all feel when we find the sweet spot in the game.

I have a recipe that sometimes helps me find this sweet spot, this zone. I like to go out on a course alone at least once every few days, even for just a few holes. I find a quiet time, and then I'm off. Inevitably, the Ballybunion feeling arrives.

One fall day I played the Royal West Norfolk course in Brancaster, England, three hours north of London in the county of Norfolk. The links sits on a spit of land beside a body of water known as The Wash. The area is renowned as a natural waterfowl site; bird watchers make pilgrimages here. The course itself is known as Brancaster for the tiny village nearby, and it's a lonely, majestic place. Golfers sometimes are marooned at the course when the tide is in. "In front of the village is a stretch of grey-green marsh,"

Bernard Darwin wrote in *The Golf Courses of the British Isles*, "and beyond the marsh is a range of sandhills, and that is where the golf is."

I arrived at Royal West Norfolk in mid-afternoon on a November day. The weather was perfect — cool, breezy, and sunny. Major Nigel A. Carrington-Smith, the club secretary, allowed me out as a single. The turf was firm, the greens fast, the course gleaming. I was in the right place and hit a long drive down the first, followed by a five-iron that I pulled slightly. But I was lucky; the ball hit a mound just left of the green and kicked down within six inches of the hole. The easy birdie put me in the zone. I could feel it.

Then I played quickly. The first nine took me an hour and five minutes. I punched shots along hollows in the fairways and into the greens, lofted mid-irons over the "sleeper" bunkers, or what we know as bunkers fortified with railroad ties. Brancaster is famous for these bunkers. I hit a high iron over the deep sleeper bunker and onto the par-three fourth, then drove my tee ball across the marsh on the eighth. I played the tenth, another par-three, with a nine-iron onto a table green and watched as my approach to the fifteenth flew over the sleeper bunker thirty yards short of the green and bounded onto the green within twelve feet of the hole. It was nearly dark as I reached the sixteenth green. I continued to strike the ball well, but bogeyed that hole and the seventeenth, then hit my second in darkness over the final green in front of the clubhouse that stands sentinel over the links. I pitched to the green twenty feet from the hole, from where I was just able to make out the hole. Two putts later I had shot seventy-six and had done so in two hours and five minutes.

This was ecstasy-inducing golf. I had the course to myself, and what a course it was. Nobody was ahead of me and nobody behind, a rare occurrence in golf. The fairways had what Bernard Darwin called "lovely turf that can put a little spring into the most leaden and depressed foot." This was autumn golf at its finest. The game was stripped to its essential elements: the course, one player, clubs, a ball, the swing. The pace was brisk, my senses awakened. This was the way to play golf, moving quickly, the senses alive, each shot a challenge. When I left I longed for more such golf. I'd confirmed I could find rapture in the game. I just had to play the game in a place and under conditions that I enjoyed. I just had to give myself the chance.

# FIVE

# Caddying:
## Along for the Ride

The professional caddie is golf's equivalent of the nomad. He wanders from course to course, searching for a home, home being any course where he might find a money-making golfer, or better, a winner. He is part of the action, talking to the ball, sweating over each shot, chatting with and encouraging his golfer. He and his golfer are partners, a team. A caddie can help a player figure the wind, pick a club, read a green. The rules of golf establish and confirm the caddie's and golfer's interdependent relationship. Rule Six deals with the player's responsibilities and the caddie's role. "For any breach of a Rule by his caddie," Rule Six, Section Four points out, "the player incurs the applicable penalty." The caddie who accidentally kicks his player's ball causes the golfer to incur a penalty. He'll feel terrible, to be sure, but the knowledge that he can cause his player such grief is the flip side of the realization that he can also assist his player. He's the only person from whom the golfer can take advice. The two are bonded, and it is upon the caddie's skill that his player's success to some degree depends. Caddies accept the possible penalties that go with the territory because they are aware that without risk there is no reward.

The rewards of caddying are exactly related to getting close to one's golfer. At the same time, that closeness is more illusory than real. The caddie exists in a peculiar relationship to his player, for, notwithstanding his duties, he lives vicariously. His livelihood depends on his golfer's performance. His feelings are often a consequence of his golfer's play. He is part of the action, but by no means is he its source. The golfer makes the final decisions. He hits the ball. The caddie can sometimes be defined as much by what he isn't to do as by what he is to do. He isn't to interfere by speaking out of turn. He isn't to allow the grips of a club to get so slick that the golfer has difficulty holding them. If his player is skittish, he isn't to exhort the ball to do one thing or another by saying "Carry the trap," or, "Catch the lip," or "Don't go there."

Unusual as the relationship is — there is no equivalent in any other sport — caddying has also been an honorable way of being involved with golf since the late seventeenth century. In *The History of Golf*, Robert Browning points out that the word "caddie" itself is the Scottish spelling of the French *cadet*, which referred to "a little chief, a title originally given to the younger sons of the French nobility who came to Edinburgh as pages in the train of Mary Queen of Scots." The term later took on a derogatory meaning, referring to boys and men who slouched about the streets of eighteenth-century Edinburgh as they waited to pick up odd jobs. Lexicographer Peter Davies wrote in his dictionary of golfing terms that many of these people might have been old soldiers who decided to call themselves "caddies," that is, gentlemen freelancers or noncommissioned officers, so as to distinguish themselves from gainfully employed private servants. The term "caddie," therefore, meant a porter. The idea of carrying was central, but it was years before it came to mean only a person who carried golf clubs.

The first caddie, in fact, seems not only to have been a person who carried clubs, but also one who had other responsibilities, namely, announcing to his player and the other golfers in the group where their golf balls had landed. This dual responsibility fell on one Andrew Dickson, who caddied in 1681 and 1682 for the Duke of York when he lived in Edinburgh and played on Leith Links just east of the city. The Duke later became King James II. Leith was the port of Edinburgh, and its soil was rather soft and boggy. The course consisted of only five holes, measuring 414, 461, 426, 495, and 435 yards respectively. A round consisted of three times round, or fifteen holes in sum.

The watery nature of the soil must have caused some golf balls to sink; all the more reason for Dickson to scoot ahead of the shots toward the landing areas in preparation for announcing their eventual location. Hence the term "fore," a contraction of "before," as in "running before." If the Duke of York were anything like the generations of golfers who followed him, he was probably incensed when Dickson couldn't find the ball. Dickson surely took his responsibilities seriously and thereby became the first true caddie: He had a stake in his player's fate. For one thing, he didn't want to incur his wrath, so he watched closely. Dickson's work must have satisfied him; he remained in golf and went on to establish a reputation as a maker of fine golf clubs. Indeed, he had made some for the Duke while serving as his caddie.

By mid-eighteenth century, the caddie was a well-established figure on Scottish golf courses. The Royal and Ancient Golf Club of St. Andrews issued regulations outlining how caddies should be paid. Caddies who went beyond The Hole o'Cross on the Old Course, now the thirteenth, were to be paid the sum of sixpence sterling as opposed to the fourpence to be paid to their colleagues who didn't go that far. Golfers who failed to pay these sums were ordered to compensate the club by way of two pint bottles of claret.

The caddie was respected. He was so much a part of the action that he was called a "professional," one who gave instruction to his player. Browning writes that in the old days the caddie was "his patron's guide, philosopher, and friend, his instructor when he was off his game, and co-arbiter with the opposition caddie in all disputes." Many caddies believed they were the intelligence of the team; they advised and the player hit the ball. Their feelings are understandable. Lives there a caddie who doesn't think he knew better than the golfer what to do on a particular shot? After all, the caddie sees the shot plain and simple. His nerves act up, but he need not silence them to play the shot. His is the voice of reason. Surely, if he were talented enough, he could hit the shot properly.

That belief is natural, and it is one reason that many top players began their careers as caddies. They learned to play by watching and by gradually becoming immersed in the game. Such stars as Chick Evans, Walter Hagen, Gene Sarazen, and Tony Lema started as caddies. It's not so much that they learned how to swing the club properly, but that they became enamored of the game. Evans, writing in 1921, said that "as soon as I possessed a golf club I kept it in my hand most of the time, and swung it in as close an imitation of the best players as was possible to me, but my method, I regret to say, was wrong, and that meant many a month of discouragement." What was important, though, was the feeling he developed for golf.

"I made a study of caddying from the beginning," Evans writes. He watched older, experienced caddies and took note of their habits. "And if I could think out anything that seemed better I did that, too. It was easy for me to learn quickly the names of all the clubs, and I noticed, too, that the members had different ways of taking them for the next shot. When they called for them I got so that, without looking, I could just feel for the right club and hand it out. Many caddies pulled out the club and thrust the cold iron into the player's hand. I made a point of dusting off the head of the club and handing the grip to the player."

This painstaking attention is the essence of caddying. It's detail work. I first felt its lure when I was twelve years old. The course was the lush York Downs Golf and Country Club, only a mile or so from my home, and I would regularly drive by with my family or cycle alongside the course. It was private, but that didn't mean I couldn't look. I sometimes visited the public Don Valley course that ran up against York Downs, and in early spring I would make my way down to the waters of the swelling Don River, hip-hugging boots protecting me. From time to time I wandered over to the edge of the Valley, as we called it, and lofted a ball into the lavish grounds of York Downs. It was my way of announcing that I wanted to be there, where the grounds were well tended, the fairways manicured, the sand raked carefully into neat furrows, and the greens smooth and fast. Caddying was my way in. I signed up.

The work wasn't always readily available. A novice, I was relegated for lengthy periods to the confines of the caddie pen, a small, crowded area near the pro shop. There I awaited a call from the caddie-master. A decent morning's work comprised one round. Carrying double was better, a bag on each shoulder, rooting for each player so that I might attract top wages from each golfer. I didn't mind going two rounds a day. One loop or two, the course was where I wanted to be. Caddies were allowed to play on Mondays. I spent the weekends planning how I'd play on Monday.

Although I hurt after two rounds and could barely make my way home, the course still was fixed in my mind's eye. It was gorgeous, a manicured retreat only a few yards from one of Toronto's main thoroughfares. One par-three crossed a valley; the other side was an arboretum of mountain ash and maple trees, a garden of golden-rod and wild raspberries. I caddied on weekends and often after school. I knew the prevailing winds; I could pick a club for a member after seeing him hit just a few shots. Sometimes I helped the golfer and sometimes I may have cost him a shot when I read a putt wrong. But I was involved, attached to the game in another way. York Downs is now a city park, but when I walk there, I see a golf course.

I was twenty-two when I decided to caddie on the pro tour. The pros were coming to the Canadian Open at the London Hunt Club, a couple of hours west of Toronto. Maybe I could pick up a bag. The job seemed appealing, hardly a job at all. Had I thought about the job description, though, I might have reconsidered. Caddying on the pro tour carried with it some of the same responsibilities as caddying for amateurs at York Downs, but it was also more difficult. Professional golfers played the game for their living. Had they provided a job description, this is how it might have read:

"Position available. Professional golfer looking for man to carry his clubs and paraphernalia six days a week in heat, rain, cold, and wind over terrain of varying elevation and composition. Said equipment weighs approximately sixty pounds. Applicant will be required to carry same for five hours a day, minimum.

"In addition to these duties on the course, the applicant must be attentive to my needs at all times, sensitive to my moods and accustomed to and willing to withstand the pressures of high-level competitive golf. When I am discouraged, he must be able to encourage me, or sometimes bear the brunt of my wrath — there being no opponent upon whom I can take out my frustration — and when I am confident, he must ensure I do not become aggressive to the point of carelessness.

"At times the applicant will be required to drive my car hundreds or thousands of miles, make my plane reservations, baby-sit my children, analyze my swing, and comfort my bleeding heart. On the course, he will ensure that my golf ball is always clean, keep my clubs free of dirt and grime, ensure that when it is raining the grips of my clubs are dry, and that I am too. He will give me the exact yardage on the golf course from any one point to any other, hand me my opponent's scorecard each three holes so that I can mark the card — without my asking him for it, hand me a new golf ball every three holes — without my asking him, never lag behind, always be mindful of the rules, and always be considerate of my fellow-competitor's play. He will offer advice when I ask for it, but otherwise refrain from engaging me in conversation. There may come a day when I feel comfortable enough with him to permit him to speak freely. But that is a goal to aspire to; for now he is to exercise extreme restraint. I am easily upset.

"The applicant must be available in case I wish to practice at any time. He must abide by the regulations of the PGA Tour for caddies. At most tournaments, he must park far from the club though I can park within fifty yards of the locker room. He must wear whatever outerwear the tournament sponsor deems appropriate (such as a T-shirt or a vest or overalls, no matter how hot it may be). He must eat in designated areas and be content with coffee and doughnuts, sandwiches at some tournaments. Above all, he must accept his background status. He must be willing to take no credit for my good play (for I, after all, hit the shots) and must accept a portion of the responsibility for my bad play (for he may be distracting me in any number of ways).

"Remuneration will be $200 weekly and six percent of my winnings, plus a bonus should I win. Applicant will pay his own expenses, including food, lodging, and travel. Apply in person to caddie area, any club on the PGA Tour, week of the event. It is crucial that the applicant be ready to work at 7:00 A.M. Monday. Employer may not show until late Tuesday or early Wednesday.''

I started in the summer of 1970 at the Canadian Open, where I had met Bob Dickson, a professional from Oklahoma who was a former United States and British Amateur champion. *Sports Illustrated* magazine had written him up in a cover story as one of the bright young stars in the game. I felt privileged to be at his side. His Oklahoma license plate read ''BIRDIE.'' I continued to caddie for Dickson a few times a year for the next six or seven years. Each summer I looked forward to his calls and was always ready to drop everything, hop into my car, and follow the Tour.

It took time to get to know Dickson on the course and to speak freely. Once, while working for him in Philadelphia, I watched as he plunked his third shot on a par-five into a stream thirty yards short of the green. He had computed the wrong yardage to the hole and so had asked for too little club. I was sure he had the wrong club, but I didn't say anything because we were just beginning our work together. I tried to convince myself that he was playing an unusual shot and so I shouldn't interfere. But the incident helped pave the way to better communication. He told me I ought to speak up if I thought he was pulling the wrong club. From then on, I felt much more a part of the game. I became a caddie, not merely a bag-toter.

Starting in 1978, I caddied for the Canadian pro Jim Nelford. He was, at the time, the country's top prospect. Nelford won the 1975 and 1976 Canadian Amateur championships and finished second in the championship in 1977, a year in which he won the highly prized U.S. Western Amateur. We met during the 1977 British Amateur at the Ganton Golf Club in Scarborough, England. He demonstrated during a practice round we played together that he had the game for the pro tours. His long game was accurate; the ball took off like a missile — the pro flight. He also possessed a deft putting touch.

I worked for Nelford at a few tournaments each season for five years. We became good friends during that period, too good sometimes. He needed to let off steam periodically, but he may have been unwilling to give me a hard time. And I may have overplayed the role of friend, philosopher, and psychologist.

Player-caddie relations are often fragile precisely because golf is so exact a sport. The mistakes are obvious, but was a poor swing the result of the caddie rustling the clubs just a second before his player settled into his stance? Or did the player lose concentration because of some aberrant thought of his own making? It's hard to tell, but it's certain that the caddie must accept his golfer's feelings while he's with him on the course. The caddie is there to listen, even if he doesn't like what he's hearing. And he'd better be sensitive to his player's temperament and habits.

At a tournament in 1981, Nelford told me to hurry, that I was lagging behind him on the course. We were out of sync. When things didn't go well, I tried to calm him down, but the words didn't always come easily. Besides, that's not always the correct approach. He said I was there to carry his clubs, not discuss his attitude. Another time I'd been suggesting he relax, that he was being hard on himself and that it could affect his shots. Then he hit an approach into a greenside trap and came out well short of the hole. He glared at me. "If you tell me to relax, I'm going to wrap this club around you." Then he slammed the head of the club into the bunker and left it there, its head buried in the sand. I should have told him to relax anyway; it was one of those times I was sure I knew better than he did what was right for him.

The 1982 Tournament Players Championship in Ponte Vedra, Florida, was one of the more taxing tournaments in which I caddied for Nelford. He was going along fine until he double-bogeyed the tenth hole in the second round to move to three over par for the tournament. Suddenly I felt every one of the sixty pounds that the bag and its contents weighed. There were sweaters, towels, golf balls, visors, medications and ointments, snacks, rain gear, wallets, yardage books, an umbrella, and fourteen golf clubs. There was also the added weight of hope and worry.

Nelford was in danger of missing the cut that would be made

after thirty-six holes to the low-seventy players and ties. Miss the cutoff and he would be down the road. This brutal fact of professional golf has no parallel in most ways of making a living, or in most other sports. A teacher doesn't lose a week's pay because he has a couple of bad days, or even a bad hour. A baseball player is paid despite pitching poorly in one game.

Nelford let me have it soon after he double-bogeyed the tenth hole at the Tournament Players Championship. He snapped at me because I was slow in cleaning his golf ball. I understood his impatience, but it still hurt. I also knew that it was my job to absorb his anger. Better he should direct it at me than take it out on his golf game. A caddie must accept whatever the golfer dishes out. That's fair enough. We crave the action. The action at this particular tournament was disappointing. Nelford missed the cut.

But caddying is not all a struggle. Who can forget Tom Watson embracing his caddie Bruce Edwards immediately after he won the 1982 U.S. Open. It was a memorable moment when Jack Nicklaus and his son Jackie Jr. embraced after Nicklaus, at age forty-six, won the 1986 Masters. Then there was the time I caddied for Nelford when he finished fourth at a Canadian tournament behind Lee Trevino, Lanny Wadkins, and Watson. The crowd gave him a standing ovation. Caddies live for these moments, and even if we don't work for players who win majors, there are many small rewards: a well-read putt that curves into the hole just when it was supposed to, an accurate club choice when the player was indecisive, a job well done no matter what the position after the tournament. No matter what happened, Nelford always said thank you when I handed him a club, gave him some tees, or acknowledged a good shot.

As a caddie, one experiences moments of sublime beauty on the golf course. Caddying is an invitation to walk with golfing virtuosos. I was sitting in the Jigger Inn beside the Road Hole at the Old Course in St. Andrews, Scotland, during the 1984 British Open, where a few caddies were enjoying some whiskey and a chip-butty — french fries on toast, the caddies' main staple. The talk, as always, was of golfers. One caddie said, "Nicklaus is definitely God 1, Watson is God 2, Palmer is God 3, Ballesteros is God 4. I got so close to Jack, I almost got religious.''

I didn't get religion, but I did feel exhilarated one evening when I learned I would be caddying the next day in a group that included Nicklaus. The tournament was the King's Island Open near Cincinnati, and Nicklaus, in his home state of Ohio, was a popular figure. He was in danger of missing the cut during the second round when suddenly he turned it on. Having driven well down the fairway of a long par-five, he faced a shot of 260 yards to carry a wide trap that protected the green. A tree fifty yards ahead on the right side of the fairway blocked him from taking a direct route to the green, but he didn't give that a thought. "I've got to make something happen," he told his caddie. Nicklaus launched a shot that soared and soared and carried the bunker and landed on the green. Two putts later he had his birdie. The cut wasn't even in question now, as it was clear he was going to make a few birdies coming in. First-hand, a few yards away, I'd seen God 1.

Trevino, too. I saw him birdie the last four holes on his way to a course record sixty-seven at the National club in Woodbridge, Ontario, while I caddied for Nelford in the 1979 Canadian PGA Championship. First, as Trevino waited to play the fifteenth hole, a par-three, he discussed what we could learn by examining a variety of divots on the tee. Each divot indicated how the golfer came through the ball. Warmed up for excellence, Trevino then played a series of mind-blowing shots, each different, each exactly what was called for: a low, slicing shot that ate up the pin on the par-three; a high lob that dropped softly short of the pin on the sixteenth, leaving him with a straight uphill birdie putt; a high slider into a tight pin position to the elevated green at the seventeenth, setting up his third consecutive birdie; a hooking runner into the eighteenth, where the green sits high on a hill.

Once, too, I saw Andy North, twice U.S. Open champion, shoot twenty-seven for nine holes. Twenty-seven. And at the 1981 Canadian Open at the Glen Abbey Golf Club in Oakville, Ontario, Nelford birdied six of the final twelve holes in the second round. I was impressed by the ease with which he was able to maneuver the ball. My duties were easy. The bag was light, far lighter than at the Tournament Players Championship. Putts were going in every one of the eight sections of the cup that pro golfers envisage: center, right center, left center; right edge, left edge; right rear, center rear, left rear. Captain Draino had shown up.

"Who's Captain Draino?" I asked Nelford.

"The Captain's a funny guy," he answered. "Sometimes he'll just sit up in the trees and tease you all day. You'll hit good putts, but the captain says no; he just won't let you make any putts. But sometimes he comes down and sits on your shoulder and smiles at you. That's when you drain everything."

I floated over the turf when Nelford played well. We looked forward to each shot. When he needed a club, I was ready with it. When, on the green, he held the ball behind him in the palm of his hand for me to clean, I was ready with the wet end of the towel. When he needed a new ball, I had it in my hand. When he needed a club, I was ready with it, the grooves cleaned of dirt, the grips washed and tacky so that he could hold the club confidently, sure it wouldn't slip. We were a team.

But caddies are also individuals. We like being thought of as team players, but we protect our independence. Most caddies aren't at all shy about dropping their player's bag on the spot if they're mistreated. We like winners, but we also have our self-respect. A rookie caddie might let himself be a punching bag for a while, but eventually he'll give as good as he gets. The players respect you then as well.

Given the nature of the job, it's not surprising that the caddies are a fraternity. They get to know each other, and before long they're easily identifiable by the nicknames they acquire. Pablo, Popeye, Cigaret, Tobacco Lou, Creamy, Dirty Dan, Golf Ball, Night Life, Disco, Professor, Killer Sam (a former boxer). They're made for the job, professional caddies all, riding roughshod across the United States on a caravan of gold one week, sleeping six to a room and saving their dimes the next. I was never a permanent fixture on the tour, but I did get a nickname while I was out there. I was Wolfman, because I had a beard.

While caddying, I could see my colleagues around the course.

We encountered each other at tees, parallel fairways, on the practice range. Here was Golf Ball, also known by his real name, Adolphus Hull. One-iron thin, he was rolling in the green in 1981 when his man, Ray Floyd, won the Doral Open and then the Tournament Players Championship. Floyd earned $367,000 for his wins, including the $250,000 bonus offered to the player who could win both. Golf Ball danced away with at least $25,000. Rumor has it that he gambled it away.

Bruce Edwards was often the leading money-winner among caddies. He worked for Tom Watson for seventeen years and made more than $40,000 in 1981, a very good living at the time. Pete Bender made more than $100,000 when he worked for Greg Norman in 1986. Angelo Argea, who was Jack Nicklaus's caddie for years, was an employee of Golden Bear Inc. and was paid every two weeks by the North Palm Beach-based company, controlled by Nicklaus. A silver-haired lanky fellow whose autograph is in demand, Angie picked up a $1,000 bonus when Nicklaus won, $2,000 if the win were a major, such as the U.S. Open or PGA Championship.

Angie worked hard. He paced the courses to get yardages from the front of the green to the pin, though pin sheets are given out prior to each round. He was also a leader of sorts. When Dave Stockton's caddie was killed in a car crash en route to the 1980 Tournament Players Championship, Angie took up a collection for the funeral. Edwards delivered the eulogy. Every caddie who had ever driven bleary-eyed all night to rendezvous with his player could imagine himself being hit by a drunk driver going the wrong way on a Florida freeway.

Unlike Angie, the majority of caddies don't work for a salary. But then they don't work for Nicklaus. They travel in groups of four, five, and six to save expenses, packing hotel rooms and eating in fast-food franchises. When you see a caddie in a fancy restaurant, you know he's just picked up a good check or has hit his employer for a loan. Old Roy Stone was well into his sixties before he left the Tour; when he was caddying, he feasted every day on a homemade beans-and-onion sandwich.

Even the well-paid caddies find that the weekly sameness saps their energies. Edwards was tiring of restaurants and motels by the time he was in his tenth year on tour. "What keeps me going," he said, "is the thrill of being in contention down the stretch." Seven years later, in 1989, Edwards was still caddying but had switched bags in a painful separation from Watson, who was gradually withdrawing from full-time play, to Norman, who felt he had at least ten good years and plenty of wins ahead of him. Edwards was now part of a true organization as well. The caddies had organized themselves into the Professional Tour Caddies' Association, the better to lobby for improved parking, more edible food, respect from tournament sponsors.

Caddies wait for a win. When it happens, they like to think they had something to do with it. Lee Lynch, who died in 1989, was still working at seventy-four, in 1982; he'd won thirty-four tournaments and had caddied for such legends as Porky Oliver, Dutch Harrison, and Ben Hogan. He once threw Hogan's clubs in the lake on the ninth hole of a tournament in Oakland. "He told me I was the goddamnedest caddie he'd seen. I wasn't going to take that."

Lynch won with Harrison, Al Geiberger, and Bobby Nichols. He also missed his share of cuts, but you could still have found him hanging around the course. It was home.

Some caddies work for television when they have the weekends off. Paul Groll, or Pablo, has caddied for Artie McNickle and Gene Littler. He's also worked for CBS, identifying the golfers for the announcers. During one stint he was in some pain; he'd been hit by a runaway cart during a pro-am at a Florida tournament.

The appeal of the itinerant caddie's life took Pablo from what he describes as a "nice life" in California. Once married, and the father of a fifteen-year-old son, he had refinished antiques and worked as a fire fighter before caddying at the Sharon Heights Country Club near Stanford University, outside San Francisco. There he caddied for Willie Mays, Tennessee Ernie Ford, and John Brodie, a former National Football League quarterback and one-time failed PGA Tour player who eventually played the Senior PGA Tour.

"Brodie convinced me to try the Tour," Pablo told me. "So I took off. I had it made in the shade, living with a nice lady and hanging out with all my radical brothers and sisters." Pablo had been involved in politics in Chicago, where he had attended North-western University in the sixties. The late Abbie Hoffman, one of the Chicago 7 who were indicted for demonstrating at the Democratic National Convention in Chicago in 1968, was a friend of Pablo's. Now Pablo has opted for a way of life that gives him the freedom conventional society cannot.

Then there's the Professor. His real name is Bradley Klein, and in his life off the course he's a research associate at Harvard University's Center for International Affairs. The Professor holds a Ph.D. in political science, has lectured all over the world, and when I last talked with him he was writing a book on the philosophical foundations of strategic studies. He's an academic scholar and a golf scholar. We met when we caddied in the 1980 Canadian Open in Montreal.

The Professor really appreciates golf. He understands its subtleties and is well versed in golf course architecture, having studied courses in many parts of the world. He even writes a column on architecture. As much a part of golf as he is, he still likes nothing better than caddying on the PGA Tour. "I envy the players' control of the ball," he tells me, "their ability to play the game the way it's meant to be played."

Klein caddied for Lon Hinkle when he shot sixty-five at Pinehurst's Number Two course during the 1977 World Golf Hall of Fame tournament. Hinkle was playing so well that on the sixteenth hole, a par-five of some 525 yards, he intentionally hit his drive into the left rough so that he could have a flier lie; that is, he'd be able to hit less club from the lie because the ball would fly from there more cleanly than from the fairway. Hinkle had 226 yards to the hole in the third round when he asked Klein what club he should use. Klein suggested a seven-iron, and when a member of ABC's television crew asked him to signal the club, Klein put two fingers down. The fellow from ABC asked, "Two-iron?" "No," Klein answered, "seven."

Caddies remember these times. As Klein points out, "It's just being there at those moments." That's why he misses caddying, now that he's got a regular job. You know that he'd like to be back on tour, even just briefly.

Ernest Caroline, or Creamy, is a good example of a caddie who still feels caddying's grip. He's in his mid-seventies, hardly the age to be carrying a sack of clubs on his back. But the tour is home to him. We chatted often as we worked the PGA Tour. He was well traveled and well used, "been up and down the ladder," as he likes to say. He worked for Arnold Palmer for years, broke up, then connected again in the late 1970s for a spell. Why is he called Creamy? Because he was going to be the best, the cream of the crop. And he was working with Arnie, the King, A.P., Numero Uno.

Creamy caddied as a kid at the Hampshire and Winged Foot clubs in Westchester County, New York. He acted in summer stock, then found himself in the Second World War, a sergeant in Gaudalcanal and the Solomon Islands. The end of the war meant the beginning of partying for Creamy. He didn't take the jobs that were offered, then when he needed a job, none was available. Eventually he tended bar and did some electrical work with his dad. That ended when his father died. He also did his share of drinking. "I was a weekend commando," he told me. "Enough boozing on the weekends to last a week. Just a rut I was in. But one day I just said to hell with it, and I quit, the boozing and the smoking. That's how I came back to caddying."

Creamy started doing a couple of loops a day near his home, making twenty to twenty-five dollars a day, decent money in the sixties. Here and there he'd work a pro-am, make a few extra bucks. Eventually he got to know Palmer's caddie, Big Blair, as Creamy calls him. "I asked him if he'd mind if I talked to Arnie. 'No, go ahead,' he said. 'I'm through.'" And so the bag was passed. Palmer always called him Ernest, never Creamy.

"It's what you make of it," Creamy said. Younger caddies, far younger, are walking by. He doesn't know many nor does he care to, but they know him. "I've done pretty well out here. You look back on your life, you ask what the hell you've done. Well, so what. Everybody does it differently."

Creamy knows that he is a lifer. Caddying is in his blood, and it's not easy for him to leave. "I wanted to be the best," he says. "And I hung on, maybe too long, like fifty years." But when he says this you know he's remembering the times he walked alongside Palmer as they won, and that he felt some of the crowd's ovation was for him. Reflected glory? Maybe, but he's also contributed. He's known as one of the best caddies for giving yardages, and, in fact, designed the original yardage books. Golfers have come to depend on these maps — tell a golfer he's got 180 to the flag when he's got 175 and he's liable to turn apoplectic.

"Lots of guys in the old days couldn't walk good yardages," Creamy points out. "Some of them had wheels that they took down the center lines of the fairways. You know the ones. They measure the yards. But I never used a wheel. I didn't think you could get good yardage with one. Besides, most of the caddies got their marks from the middle of the fairway. I'd tell them that was great if they were caddying for Hogan. But most golfers go right and left, all over the lot. You need a yardage from other places besides the middle. It was insurance. That's what you needed. They used to kid me that I'd have a yardage from the ladies' room. Sure, you never know, you might be over there. As long as you make a little map, put it down, it's there. Most everybody I worked for would go with what I had. That was my forte in the old days."

But that was years ago. Caddying has changed. Golfers now have their own yardage books, and they're perfect. The players go over them during practice rounds in case changes have been made from the last time they played the course. Check any pro golfer's den or office at home and you'll find yardage books from every course he's played. They're guidelines; his job is to plot his way around the course according to the best strategy. He picks his Point A and tries to advance the ball to Point B. The caddie need only watch it land and get there no later than his player. That's not very satisfying. The whole point of caddying is to be involved.

But caddying as a profession has its own built-in life span, at least for most people. The longer I caddied, the more I realized that I wasn't as involved as I once was. But I didn't realize what was going on until years later, when I talked with Mike Reasor. He'd caddied in the 1966 U.S. Open for Arnold Palmer.

I had the opportunity to chat with Mike Reasor in mid-1989, when he was in Toronto to play in a Canadian Tour event. I'd been wanting to meet him since 1966, when I watched the U.S. Open on television from the Olympic Club in San Francisco. Reasor's experience with Palmer was unforgettable. I remember the tournament because it encompassed in its last nine holes all the emotions that caddying could bring. The 1966 U.S. Open convinced me that one day I would like to caddie on the professional golf tour, but in retrospect, I think I also sensed in that tournament the reasons that caddying could never be a lifelong enterprise for me, and why it might one day cease to be even a part-time hobby. It took nearly a quarter-century to understand what had both appealed to and repelled me while watching the 1966 U.S. Open unfold. The tournament has gone down in golfing history. Palmer led Billy Casper by seven shots with nine holes to play. But he shot thirty-nine the final nine to Casper's thirty-two, then lost the tournament the next day in an eighteen-hole play-off. Reasor, then a college student, was at Palmer's side.

Reasor was a member of the Brigham Young University golf team, along with Johnny Miller. The team had played a college tournament at Olympic, and club member Johnny Swanson told the golfers that they were welcome to caddie during the Open if they so desired. The golfers were then obliged to use caddies that the club provided, rather than bringing their own. Reasor had only to register to caddie and the job would be his. His real interest was in playing the tournament, but he couldn't afford the entry fee for a qualifying round in Salt Lake City. Miller could, and he qualified and eventually finished ninth as an amateur. Reasor did the next best thing; he caddied.

Like all the caddies, Reasor didn't know for whom he would work. The club filled a huge hollow ball with numbered Ping-Pong balls. Each player drew a number as he arrived. Reasor waited in the caddie bin from Saturday to Monday but, it seemed, to no avail.

Number after number was drawn, but his hadn't come up. About ten-thirty on Monday morning, though, an announcement came over the loudspeaker. "Number 148," Reasor remembered, "my number, had been drawn by Arnold Palmer."

Reasor was thrilled. Palmer, then thirty-six, had won more than fifty PGA Tour events, along with seven major championships. He was a golfing legend, the man everybody watched and admired. Caddying for him as a result of a blind draw was a stroke of good fortune for Reasor. He started to walk to the clubhouse to confirm his appointment as soon as his number was drawn. But he was intercepted on the way.

"Palmer's regular caddie came out of the bushes and asked for my number," Reasor said. "I told him he'd get it over my dead body and kept walking. He was much bigger than me and could have grabbed it, but I made it past him."

Reasor remembers the 1966 U.S. Open as if he had played it himself. The final nine holes and the play-off are especially vivid. Palmer made bogey after bogey that nine while Casper made up ground with birdies. I was shocked as I watched on television. What was happening? Could Reasor help? Both he and Palmer were concerned, but something almost inexorable was happening. The center wasn't holding. Still, Palmer wasn't out of it.

Palmer and Casper were tied as they stood on the eighteenth tee to play the seventy-second hole, the last one of regulation play. Palmer drove into the heavy, deep rough left of the fairway. The lie appeared impossible.

"I looked at the ball," Reasor said, "and it didn't take much to figure out that if I were playing, I'd take a sand wedge and beat it back to the fairway."

But that wasn't Palmer's style. He went for shots no matter how difficult they were. He had 127 yards to carry the bunker in front of the long, narrow, elevated green. I can still see the wicked slash he took at the ball, the massive swath of turf that he tore out of the ground and that came flying out, the ball that just carried the trap and rolled to the back of the green. Palmer faced a downhill, thirty-foot putt and managed to get down in two for his par. Casper also parred, and they went into the eighteen-hole play-off the next day. Casper won after Palmer took a three-shot lead into the last nine holes. Reasor saw every shot.

Following the play-off, Reasor carried Palmer's clubs into the empty locker room. He got Palmer a cold beer, then sat on the end of a bench to wait for him. Palmer was attending the presentation ceremony, which was carried to the locker room by loudspeaker.

"I couldn't believe what I heard," Reasor recalled. "He was talking about me, what a good job I'd done. And more than that, he was accepting his loss with class and dignity."

Palmer then walked into the locker room, head held high, determined not to show outsiders how he was feeling. But Reasor was an insider.

"The minute he walked by the security cop at the door," Reasor said, "I could see his chin sag. When he got to the door, the first thing he did was put his arm around me and say, 'Sorry, Mike.'"

Palmer knew that Reasor had taken the loss personally. He also knew that Reasor felt for him. Such is the caddie's state of mind, and the player's as well. Each feels a double loss or a double gain, depending on the outcome. Feelings run deep. There's often little to say. The golf has said it all.

I felt many losses and a few successes during my caddying days. As time passed, I began to realize that the weight of the life a caddie leads tilts inevitably and exclusively to the vicarious. I felt happy or sad because of somebody else's fate and internalized his performance. As close as I felt to the action, I was just along for the ride. That conclusion is inescapable, but does not diminish the thrill I felt at being there. Still, to think otherwise is to delude oneself, to lead a false life, somebody else's life. That is the fundamental problem with caddying. Another person defines a caddie's identity.

Reasor caddied that one time and never again. He went on to play the PGA Tour for ten years and later worked as a director of golf at a municipal course in Seattle and at a club near Palm Springs. His next assignment was as a teaching pro in the same area, while he also participated in golf outings for corporation executives. At forty-six, while playing the Canadian Tour and other events, he was considering trying the Senior PGA Tour after he turned fifty. But he knew that nothing would ever replace his memories of the

1966 U.S. Open — its highs and lows, what Palmer showed him, what Palmer gave him.

"You can live a long time and never see a man's guts right in front of you like that," he told me. "It was the darnedest thing, the whole last day, like water running through your fingers, the biggest blowup in the history of the game. But it became a real inspiration for me, the way Palmer handled himself, how he treated people."

I also learned from golfers I worked for and from seeing others at close range, in victory and defeat, when their guts were on the line and they came through, and when they fell apart. Reasor saw it all in one intensely felt round. It took me six years before I saw enough.

While caddying, I wandered from city to city and course to course, a nomad following the tour and other men's fortunes. I loitered about for too many hours on too many courses, waiting for somebody to show up, for something to happen. I thrived on the excitement and the possibility inherent in every tournament and in every shot. The ups and downs of the life appealed to me; you couldn't have one without the other. But there were too many long evenings that I spent in foul motels, greasy meals that I should have avoided, endless lousy movies in too many strip malls in too many cities that I didn't take the time to know. One man's golf was all that I cared about, but in the end I realized I couldn't do much about his golf, and that his life wasn't mine.

I first caddied to get inside the game. And I did. But it was no longer possible as a professional caddie to enjoy carrying the bag day in and day out. Tournament sponsors insisted that caddies act as advertising banners for them. At an event in New York I was told to wear a heavy caddie vest in hot, steamy weather because the sponsor's name was on the back of the uniform. I declined the offer, but my player, Bob Dickson, was warned that he would be fined if I weren't wearing it by the time he reached the televised holes. Caddying became a job, a burden. I still was excited every time we walked onto the first tee of a tournament, and I still enjoyed watching many of the best golfers in the game. I was still walking with the golfing gods, but the romance had gone. The gods were mortal. They, too, failed more than they succeeded.

I knew my days as a caddie were over as I walked the last few holes of the 1982 Walt Disney World Golf Classic in Orlando, Florida. I felt the weight of the bag subside as Jim Nelford holed a six-foot birdie putt on the last hole to shoot sixty-five and assure himself a place on the 1983 PGA Tour. I'd been inside the ropes, but now it was over. Caddying was one way to learn the game, but it was only one link among many, and never meant to last a lifetime.

# SIX

# Around the World in Eighteen Holes

Henry Longhurst was golf's most admired writer and television broadcaster during the middle of this century. Longhurst wrote a column for London's *Sunday Times*, and what a marvelous piece of work it was: stylish and erudite, sharp-tongued where necessary, and always in touch with the mood of the game. Longhurst had a philosophy of life that was once called "gap-filling" — go anywhere and do anything that you haven't done before. "All my life I have gone on the principle of trying anything once," Longhurst wrote in 1955. "I have always thought of it to myself as 'filling in chapters.'" He followed this notion and made the golf world his territory. British journalist Mark Wilson wrote that golf was Longhurst's highway through life, and by all accounts he took a most scenic and exciting route. Longhurst called his autobiography *My Life and Soft Times*, and although he knew his share of hard as well as soft times, he chose to dwell on the latter. Golf took him around the world, and he took his readers with him.

I mention Henry Longhurst here because I am thinking of his comment that golf is the Esperanto, or universal language, of sport. Who would know better than Longhurst, since he traveled the world while following the game? He knew that golf is *the* international sport, played on all continents by nearly all people and in nearly all cultures and societies. He, more than any one golf personality, brought the global aspects of the game home to me, for it was while watching the 1962 Masters on television that I first heard Longhurst from the booth above the sixteenth green. Arnold Palmer required two birdies in the final three holes to tie Gary Player and Dow Finsterwald. Palmer's five-iron tee shot on the sixteenth, that loveliest of par-threes over a pond to a green set in a corner of pine trees and flowering bushes, finished just beyond the back right corner of the green, forty-five feet from the hole.

Longhurst said the following words, or something very close: "He has a most difficult shot from here. He'll do well to hole in two for his par." Palmer played a delicate pitching wedge that seemed to run forever down the slope toward the hole. Longhurst didn't say a word, as he was not one to talk on the stroke. When the ball dropped into the hole on its last roll, however, Longhurst did speak. "And there you have it," he said. And that was all. Palmer went on to win.

Those words brought the essence of golf home for me. There was no telling what might happen on any shot. Somehow Longhurst's words impressed themselves upon me as the most sophisticated analysis of the game I had heard. It occurred to me for the first time that golf was truly a game for the world; after all, I was listening to an Englishman describe a shot hit by an American at one of the world's two or three most beautiful courses. I couldn't have known it then, but I believe that Longhurst's words, having imprinted themselves upon my golfing mind, were a beacon to me to follow the game, and to try to understand it. An Englishman at Augusta suggested that golf could take you anywhere.

I have found this to be true, because golf crosses so many borders. Wandering players can get a game anywhere, because there are courses everywhere. Moreover, the game's popularity is reflected in places one normally doesn't associate with it. Once, for instance,

I wandered into Gallery 1900-2000 in Paris and found an exhibition called Retro-Sport, 1850-1940, in which owner Marcel Fleiss had included many examples of golf art and curios. Another time, I was on a train to Copenhagen when I met Sven-Age Sletback, a team handball player whose true passion was golf although he had been playing but three years and had achieved only a twenty-five handicap. Then there was the time a service organization in Tel Aviv assigned me to the Sdot Yam kibbutz; the kibbutz bordered Caesarea, Israel's only golf course.

Golf is neither an American nor a British nor a Japanese nor an Australian game. It's caught the fancy of people all the world over, though they might have widely differing political views and economic systems. But golf suits them. John Lantang was teaching golf thirteen hours a day at Senayan, a government sports complex in Jakarta, when I visited there. His *khusus sekolan golf* — special school for golf — was full the evening I visited. Lantang said, "I think golf is a very good game for the Indonesians. We are a philosophical people, and in golf you have much philosophy. I tell my students golf is like your own life line. At first, you will not notice your own mistake. Later, you will learn."

Golf crosses borders because the only language required is a body language. Make a swing and you'll make contact — with the ball, one hopes, but also with other golfers. I've played rounds with people where we hardly spoke a word because we didn't have a common verbal language. But the hours on the course and the game's joys and frustrations brought us closer to one another. Goodwill was fostered.

It is for these reasons that international competition is so popular. The World Amateur Golf Council includes the governing bodies of golf in more than sixty countries. There's the Burma Golf Federation and the Fiji Golf Association; the Indian Golf Union and the Israeli Golf Federation; the Golf Union of Iceland and the Trinidad and Tobago Golf Association. Golfers from many of these countries have been meeting in even years since 1958 in the World Amateur Team Championship, which is open to men and women.

A similar situation exists at the professional level. The major men's Tours are in the United States, Japan, and Europe, with lesser tours elsewhere. The situation in women's golf is similar. Male professionals gather biennially, in odd years, to compete in the Ryder Cup, a competition between teams of twelve from the United States and Europe. Numerous other international events include many more professionals from many more countries.

These competitions take place partly because golf is the same game all over the world. The rules of golf as set forth by the United States Golf Association and The Royal and Ancient Golf Club of St. Andrews — the two major organizing bodies of the game — allow only for minor variations that do not affect the playing of the game. A course consists of eighteen holes. The hole is 4¼" in diameter. Fourteen clubs are allowed, no more. The golfer who tees off at the Old Course in St. Andrews, Scotland, plays the same game as the player who starts out at Royal Calcutta in India. The handicapping system whereby people are graded according to their abilities enables them to compete against one another; hence the worldwide custom of figuring out a game on the first tee. Golfers the world over kid around on first tees everywhere, trying to secure an advantage that honestly computed handicaps prevent. Then they go off on their appointed rounds, wondering what will happen.

As consistent as the rules of golf are from country to country, the game still differs from country to country, region to region, club to club. Golf transcends cultural differences, but at the same time allows for cultural variation. To travel in the world of golf is to observe the myriad ways in which human beings can express the game. As Henry Longhurst observed, "Golf is just about the best excuse for travel yet discovered. It gives you a purpose in the background, brings you in touch with the most influential and amusing of the natives, and gives you plenty of time for activities other than the golf."

## JAPAN

Tokyo is the busiest city I've visited, and Japan the most congested country. It's hard to find room in this country where 100,000,000 people live in a land only slightly larger than California. The United States is twenty times larger than Japan, but has only two and a half times as many people. The lack of open space in Japan means that there aren't many courses, some 1,200 as opposed to more than 10,000 in the United States. Japan has one course for every 8,333 golfers. The United States has one for every 1,352 golfers. But the relative lack of courses doesn't stop the Japanese from being obsessed with the game. There is so much interest in golf that private club memberships go for as much as $2,000,000 and are traded on the open market as transferable shares. A company called Eagle Golf Services located in Tokyo's Ohtemachi Building in a major commercial area exists solely to buy and sell memberships on behalf of its clients. Course memberships are in demand, as are playing times at the few available public courses. Land for courses is so scarce in Japan that some courses are carved out of mountains and play from level to level. Some courses maintain a "thunderbolt bus" on the course to bring golfers back to the clubhouse in case of a storm, precisely because they may find themselves in a region of the course that makes walking back quickly impossible.

There may be relatively few courses in Japan, but the game is still popular. There are 3,500 driving ranges, three weekly golf papers, and five monthly magazines. A national election was being held when I visited the country. There was golf on television from morning until early afternoon. Later, when election results started to come in, TV Tokyo showed United States teaching professional Gary Wiren giving lessons through an interpreter to two Japanese women.

While visiting Japan, I met Tak Kaneda, an advertising executive who also was writing a weekly newspaper column on golf, zen, and business, called "Green Salon." He takes me one night to Shiba Golf, a triple-tiered driving range that is packed night after night with golf-crazed Japanese. Shiba Golf must be the world's largest driving range. Located on the site of a former temple, Shiba Golf's three tiers rise in a half-moon in front of a spacious, grassy field. There's room here.

Entering Shiba, I sign up at the front desk and am given a card to insert into a machine near my designated tee. Information about how many balls I've hit will be fed from the machine to central station and the cost calculated. I hit forty balls off rubber mats from the middle tier and watch as they take off into the Tokyo night.

While I hit the balls, Kaneda tells me a story that helps explain the Japanese passion for golf. "It's the story of the armor bug," Kaneda says. "The children in Japan play with this bug, but when it dies, they say, 'Daddy, the bug has run out of batteries.'"

Kaneda makes his point. The Japanese live in an industrialized culture on a small island. They are removed from nature, a separation that even children feel. Hence their appreciation of golf. Hence their willingness to endure long lineups even at driving ranges, where they often must pre-book starting times. This is also why they turn a round of golf into a celebration replete with food, sake, ritual baths after the round, and dinner. We meet for breakfast, then stop after a few holes for a snack of corn soup or miso soup at one of the resting places on the course. Between nines we have lunch, having booked a starting time for the back nine. It doesn't matter if the day's golf takes just that long — a day. Golf is meant to take the Japanese person away from his usual environment and his normal bustling habits. It's a day away, the Japanese equivalent of an American's outing in the country after a week's work in Manhattan.

"A Japanese person's space is increased when he plays golf," Kaneda continues. "In Tokyo or Osaka we live in such confinement. So when we play on the golf course, we have a good feeling. We see the beautiful sky. On a golf course, the Japanese feel for the first time that they are living."

A few days in Japan convinces me that Kaneda's assessment is accurate. While there, I visit one place in particular where the golf obsession is obvious. It's a cold night before Christmas, the season in Japan of *bohnen-kai*, forgetting the year's troubles, and I visit the rooftop driving range of the Maruzen department store on the Ginza, Japan's glitzy main shopping street. I take the elevator to "R" for roof, and there I find an area so large that I can aim in various directions. Cars speed by on highways that seem to leap-frog above the streets below, but I hardly notice them. My attention is on a bull's-eye suspended in the mesh of the driving net. The sum of 700 yen, about three dollars, gets me two dozen balls and a driver. I feel free up on the roof, whereas just a few minutes ago I was in a human traffic jam. Now I am alone. A few golfers join me presently, but we don't speak, just smile and hit our golf balls. We celebrate *bohnen-kai* in our own way, by hitting balls and feeling unencumbered.

I stay for thirty minutes, feeling I'm golfing at the center of the world. I'm above it all — the noise, the crowds, the traffic, the commerce. I can see the sky and fully appreciate what golf means to the Japanese. I feel delivered, golfing on the roof of a department store in Tokyo.

## *INDONESIA*

I am visiting Indonesia for the World Cup, a tournament for two-man teams of professionals. My assignment is to cover the event in Jakarta, after which I will journey to Bali, "the magical island at the end of the world," as I recall a magazine article referring to it. In Jakarta I will see the Pondok Indah golf club, and then the Jagorawi club an hour outside of the city. Bali Handara awaits me after the tournament, an hour's flight away and then a couple of hours' drive north into higher, cooler ground.

Walking Pondok Indah, I get a sense of the game in Indonesia. It is, above all, a game in a garden. Things grow quickly. Put a fence up, the story goes, and vegetation will cover it in a week.

It's the rainy season in Indonesia, but World Cup tournament officials don't seem concerned. They have hired three *pawang*, or rainstoppers. The *pawang* don't eat, sleep, or drink for three days before the tournament, the better to work themselves into a rain-stopping frenzy. During the event itself, they chant and perform incense ceremonies. They admit that if it were raining throughout Indonesia, they couldn't prevent the rain from falling on Pondok Indah. But they can divert imminent storms from Pondok Indah to areas in Indonesia where it's dry.

Clouds have gathered, and the sky is darkening. The vice president of Indonesia speaks at the official opening of the World Cup while thunder claps all around. It's dry for the moment, but it starts to pour as soon as he leaves. There's no rain during the tournament itself.

Pondok Indah introduces me to the richness of the game in Indonesia, its colors and fragrances. Moslems living just off the course are chanting as I enter the property. *Bibi*, or "aunts," greet me on the course. These smiling women of all ages are clad in long, colorful skirts and conical hats made from coconut leaves. Their job is to keep the course clean using bamboo shoots to sweep away any debris. Meanwhile, children sit on fences that border the course's opening holes, chattering away and always friendly. There's the smell of *kretek*, the clove cigarettes that Indonesians smoke, and on the fifth hole, the flaming red leaves of the flamboyans trees, as they're known. I walk the course on my own one early evening, welcoming the gifts that the environment offers. Soon I will find other gifts at the Jagorawi Golf and Country Club.

Jagorawi is also known as Jagorawi Golf Gardens. It's a naturalist's paradise, a revelation whose holes are set on a series of terraces amidst sculptured hills and rice fields. Jagorawi (literally, the road from Jakarta to Bogor, location of the enchanting gardens behind the Presidential Palace) begins with a first tee that sits at least 150 feet above a fast-running stream, then descends to a flat plain that describes the opening fairway. The fairway is edged as if by an X-acto knife, so sharp are its outlines as it tumbles into wild vegetation on either side. The course was built entirely by hand — the hands of natives who removed earth in baskets that they hung from bamboo poles and slung across their shoulders.

The best parts of Jagorawi are the views and the walks up and down gentle hills to the terraced fairways. I'm in a golfing greenhouse one moment, an oxygenated peak the next. To the east of the ninth hole I can see from one level of the sculpted fairway to the black top of an inactive volcano. At the fifteenth hole, a 465-yard par-five that bends around and above the rice fields below, I play my drive to the left to avoid the deep, fertile canyons where I might hit one of the women who stand knee-deep in the mud of the rice beds. Children swing from tree branches, while others bathe in the streams. Jagorawi is alive.

There are also some views that last forever in the mind's eye. En route from the sixteenth green to the seventeenth tee, I notice rock gardens set on islands in small streams, and a series of miniature waterfalls. I feel as if I'm in a trance state by the time I reach the last few holes. But there's more to come at Bali Handara.

Pondok Indah, a course built in the 1970s, was constructed by modern earth-moving machinery, and Jagorawi was chiseled by human hands, but Bali Handara was "discovered," as old-timers in Scotland like to say of the Old Course in St. Andrews. Bali Handara is a jewel of the golfing world. Peter Thomson, the Australian who is a five-time British Open champion and a member of the firm that built Jagorawi and Bali Handara, calls it a "hideaway."

Bali Handara lies tranquilly in a bowl at the foot of a tropical rain forest 4,000 feet above sea level in the mountains. Surveying the course late one afternoon, I'm surrounded by dense forest that soars seemingly ever upwards and is home to monkeys and deer, not to mention the many golf balls that must have come to rest here, driven from the tee of the 572-yard final hole that plunges from that high tee at the edge of the woods to the floor of the course.

A grayish mist settles over the treetops as I play. To the south, the treetops sweep away in a neat curve, as if some elegant force of nature has clipped their broad surfaces into a crew cut. Behind me, the sun that will plummet out of the Indonesian sky at exactly 6:00 P.M. hangs suspended over a mountain lake called Buyan. I can hear Hindus chanting from the neighboring village of Pencasari and can see their homes and tended fields beyond the lake. The soothing music of a flute caresses the soft air.

I've already had quite an afternoon on this course that was once a dairy and coffee plantation. Accompanied by Suaning, a caddie from the village, I had played my way through the early holes without distinguishing myself. Still, the shots had an aura given them by the splendor of the environment. Mountains loomed in the distance as I played, creating that delicious moment when the ball seemed to hang in the sky against the background before diving to the ground.

Shortly thereafter I made a hole in one on the 180-yard fourth hole. Suaning advised me to use a six-iron, and so I did. The ball drifted just slightly left to right, as I hoped it would, hit behind the hole and spun back in. Suaning marked my scorecard carefully, inscribing the number 1 inside a triangle, as if I had just been ordained into a secret fraternity. A crowd had gathered to

congratulate me by the time we reached the perimeter of the course
a few holes later. Suaning had gotten the word out, but I didn't
know how.

I soon forgot about the hole in one, however, as Bali Handara's
grandeur unfolded. There were the reds, greens, blues, and yellows
of the flowering bushes; the reverse teardrop green at the ninth;
the tall, slim cemarililin, a tree that marked points 150 yards from
the green; the belenging, a tiny green beetle on the thirteenth green;
a black and yellow striped butterfly that fluttered around the sixteenth tee; the view from the raised seventeenth tee back to the
clubhouse and its red-tiled roof 1,000 yards away; the cottages in
a park beyond, where I was staying; and a party that the club threw
for me upon the occasion of my hole in one.

After that party, I took one last walk down the final fairway.
It's dusk, and I'm the last golfer on the course, three clubs in my
arms, a couple of golf balls to use, my mind quiet. I'm 12,000 miles
from home, my shadow is twelve paces long, and I can feel the breeze
that slides out of the forest and freshens the air with a pine scent.

Moments later I putt out on the eighteenth green and think of
what Peter Thomson had told me about Pondok Indah, Jagorawi,
and Bali Handara — the three faces of Indonesian golf. "Pondok
Indah is a high-class course, and Jagorawi is spectacular. But Bali
Handara is heavenly, a special beauty."

*RUSSIA*

I have never been to the Soviet Union, but golf may one day take
me there, too. At the same time, it's difficult at first to reconcile
golf in the Soviet Union with the politics of the country, notwithstanding the present changes. There is, after all, a view that golf is a
rich man's game that represents the worst excesses of capitalist
culture. It seems the paradigm of a wealth-conscious, result-oriented
society. The game can be expensive to play, and all anybody seems
to care about is his score. Above and beyond all this, it's an
individual sport. Group thinking and the idea of the common good
for the common man don't seem to have much place in golf.

But golf also has other themes — themes more genuine and central
to the game. In its original incarnation, it wasn't a sport where score

and score alone counted, where a person set out to see what kind of a number he could post. Instead, he engaged another golfer in match play, a one-on-one contest over eighteen holes. They were involved with one another more directly than in medal play, where total score counts and where you don't play an individual so much as you play the scorecard. They also socialized and got to know one another well over the course of their round. There was a spirit of togetherness.

Golf's handicap method allows this. Players of differing abilities can compete with one another. There's a certain egalitarianism about the enterprise. I can have a game with Jack Nicklaus as long as he gives me enough shots during the round.

Golf is also a sport for people who like the outdoors and enjoy walking, notwithstanding the intrusion of golf carts into the game. Golf carts benefit the elderly and people who for whatever reason are unable to walk. They have no place in real golf, though, and real golfers don't take carts. They walk.

It's obvious, then, that golf's vices are its virtues looked at from another point of view. Many people ride, but walking is at the heart of the game. Many people play for the score, but many others play for the pleasure and the company of friends; many also turn golf into a team sport by participating in better-ball or alternate shot events. And every golfer who plays the game can establish a legitimate handicap; some golfers abuse the principle and establish false handicaps so that they can win money while wagering on matches or win prizes in tournaments, but the majority play by the book. And the book shows that golf is a game for the masses. It's reasonable to think that the game could catch on in the Soviet Union, especially with the current move toward a more democratic system.

And catch on it might, because the Republic's first government-sanctioned, eighteen-hole course is under construction. The Nachabino course is being built twelve miles away from Moscow's city center, as part of the Nachabino Sports Complex. It's the result of fifteen years of collaboration and political intrigue that involved Armand Hammer, the American businessman-diplomat who has long served as a conduit to the Soviets; golf architect Robert Trent Jones, Jr.; and the Soviets themselves. The Soviets have already expressed interest in holding the World Amateur Team Championship. Who knows, we might one day see a U.S.S.R. Open, a Jack Nicholas instead of a Czar Nicholas.

But this is getting ahead of the story. How did the course come about? What went on? For the answers, I sought out Robert Trent Jones, Jr., the California-based course designer who considers the job of designing the Soviet Union's first course the plum assignment of his career.

Jones has designed courses on submerged rice paddies in Thailand and out of the side of a Swiss mountain. He has wide political connections, having worked in the United States on behalf of Corazon Aquino when she was involved in her successful campaign to become president of the Philippines in 1986. Jones is an occasional golfing partner of Georgia senator Sam Nunn, who was spoken of as a Democratic Party candidate for the 1988 presidential election. He's a fine player, and he's got the kind of ambition one needs to even get to the point of talking about building the Soviet Union's first course.

But Jones couldn't have gotten anywhere in the Soviet world without Hammer, who set the process in motion. In 1974 Hammer used his extensive contacts in the Soviet Union to argue that not only would a course near Moscow serve the international community, but that the Soviets might also take to the game. He reasoned that because golf was both an individual and a team game, it might serve as a link between capitalism and communism. He knew that the handicap system was at the core of the game and figured such egalitarianism would appeal to the Soviets. Arguments were put forth that golf suited the common man. Somebody told me that the Soviet Union's official paper, *Pravda*, published an article demonstrating that golf was a game for the proletariat.

While Hammer thought about a course and worked on laying the philosophical foundations for one, Jones was also contemplating golf in the U.S.S.R. He had visited Russia in the early 1960s and felt the game would go well there. Jones became seized with the idea on a trip to Moscow in 1974 when he met Vladimir Kuznetsov, who had learned golf while serving as Soviet ambassador to Malaysia.

The two had a conversation that, to hear Jones tell it, was right out of P.G. Wodehouse's story *The Clicking of Cuthbert*. Wodehouse introduces the fictional character Vladimir Brusiloff, who, the story goes, once played against Lenin and Trotsky at a course called Nijni-Novgorod. Kuznetsov and Jones spoke as if they were present at Nijni-Novgorod.

"You play golf?" Ambassador Kuznetsov asked Jones.

"Yes," Jones answered.

"What is your handicap?"

"Oh, about a six," Jones said.

"Well," the ambassador countered, "that's pretty good. I'm a fourteen myself."

"Really," Jones said. "Where do you play?"

"Ah," the ambassador sighed, "that is the only problem. I must go to Czechoslovakia on my vacation to play. They have courses there."

Jones decided then and there that he would one day build a course in the Soviet Union. The Soviets said they would look for suitable land, but they had no idea of how much land was needed. Jones visited Moscow a couple of times in the next few years to look for land. By 1979, a site had been approved and the Soviets had provided an accurate map of the land from which Jones could design the course. But later that same year, the Soviets invaded Afghanistan and the project went into a deep freeze. Only when Mikhail Gorbachev introduced Glasnost in the mid-1980s was the idea revived. It was a fresh spring. The Soviets were willing to talk about the project again.

By the summer of 1987, Jones had visited Moscow many times. He'd enlisted Senator Nunn's help, but there was still plenty of work to be done. Jones went to Washington a week before the Summit that was held December 8 to 10, 1987, where U.S. President Ronald Reagan and Gorbachev were to meet.

Senator Nunn and Soviet Deputy Foreign Minister Boris Chaplin had dinner together in Washington. Chaplin didn't know a birdie from a bogey or an iron from an iron curtain. But he warmed to the idea of a course in the U.S.S.R. Nunn mentioned the idea to Gorbachev during lunch at the Summit. Gorbachev had no idea what golf was all about, but he listened and was open to the idea.

Jones visited Moscow after the Washington Summit to inspect the proposed site for the course. The Soviets had already checked him out carefully, and back home in the United States he was called upon to assure the powers that be that he and his associates wouldn't be giving away technological secrets to the Soviets by building a course. The next item on the agenda was a visit in June 1988 to the Moscow Summit. The Soviets had said they would make an official announcement that the Nachabino course was on. Jones and his associate, lawyer Blake Stafford, holed up in the Minsk Hotel. They awaited a call from the Soviets. It didn't seem to be in the offing.

"Jones thought it was going to be put on the shelf," Stafford remembered. "The Soviet Foreign Ministry people were occupied entertaining Reagan. Bobby was deflated, very discouraged. He felt that the thing wasn't going to make it. No preparations had been made for the announcement."

But then the phone rang in Jones's room in the Minsk Hotel. Nachabino had been put on the agenda for June 1. Documents would be signed, an announcement made.

Hammer and Jones arrived at the formal Summit Hall in Moscow's Sobin Center at the appointed hour of 5:00 P.M. An announcement was made that construction would soon begin on the U.S.S.R.'s first eighteen-hole course, run by the government for the people and free to Soviet citizens. Hammer had donated $150,000 to offset initial hard currency costs. He wanted to be known as the founder of the first course in the Soviet Union. Jones wanted to be known as the designer of the first course in the Soviet Union.

The deal was confirmed. Construction began soon after, and the Soviets awaited their first course.

"The Soviets like the idea of golf being a lifetime game," Jones told me. "They also like the handicap system because it equalizes all golfers so that nobody will be embarrassed. The game fits in with the egalitarian view. It's also not lost on the Soviets that St. Andrews in Scotland and St. Basil's Cathedral in Moscow are on the same latitude. Personally, I find the Russians a very proud and warm people. Theirs is an agrarian society. Golf fits in. They are physically healthy and strong, an athletic people. When I go over there they ask me to come and pick mushrooms in the forest."

As golfers, the Soviets will be looking for golf balls, not mushrooms, in the forest. Nachabino will be built in a pine forest, and lakes will come into play on the 7,000-yard course. But the course won't be exceptionally difficult. It's meant to encourage the Soviets to take up the game. Should they do so, and there's every reason to think they will, that U.S.S.R. Open may well take place by the millenium.

### GREAT BRITAIN

Perhaps the most famous date in golf's early history is March 14, 1457, and not because somebody made three holes in one during a round, broke a course record, or won a major championship. Instead, the date is well known because it was then that golf was banned by an act of Scottish Parliament, a decree that not only shows how popular the game was, but also establishes its ancestral home — Scotland — and indicates that it began more than 500 years ago. Before 1457 there was no mention anywhere of golf, and then suddenly, there it is in an Act of Parliament.

But why would King James II want to ban the populace from playing the game? The answer is simply that it was so popular it was getting in the way of the normal business of the day, that is, defending the country. So it was that it was decreed that "the futeball and golfe be utterly cryed downe and not to be used." The ban continued through the following two reigns in Scotland and in 1491 read as follows: "It is statute and ordained that in na place of the Realme there be used Fute-ball, Golfe, or uther sik unproffitable sportis," because they were contrary to "the commoun good of the Realme and defense thereof."

Military considerations or not, golf lasted and was from the days of its beginnings a game for all people, all classes, royalty and public servant, businessman and child. Robert Browning in *A History of*

*Golf* points out that from 1502 until 1688, every reigning monarch in the Stuart line — two kings and one queen of Scotland, four kings of the United Kingdom — was a golfer. Cobblers and tailors also played, and it was only a matter of time until they formed clubs, by which were meant not necessarily golf courses, but societies of golfers who gathered to play over a course. The first such club was started in 1744, when "several Gentlemen of Honour, skilfull in the ancient and healthfull exercise of Golf," petitioned the City of Edinburgh to come up with a Silver Club for annual competition on Leith Links, five holes in the port of Leith east of the city. There is general agreement that this was the beginning of what would become the Honourable Company of Edinburgh Golfers, a name that their successors retain, except that they now play at the Muirfield Golf Club. Muirfield is further along the road east of Edinburgh, and although it is a private club dominated by the Honourable Company, it is also open to visitors. This is in the ancient tradition of golf being a game for everybody. Muirfield isn't the easiest course to get on if you're not a member, but non-members do have playing privileges at certain times.

Ten years after the Leith golfers got together to form their club, the Royal and Ancient Golf Club of St. Andrews was started. Twenty-two "Noblemen and Gentlemen, being admirers of the ancient and healthful exercise of the Golf," met on May 14, 1754, to play for their own Silver Club. They had already drawn up the first rules of golf, known as "Articles and Laws in playing the Golf." The rules were meant to govern the conduct of the match and were drawn up for match play rather than stroke play. Nevertheless, the thirteen rules contain much that has lasted, for instance, Rule Ten, which points out that "if a ball is stop'd by any person, horse, dog or anything else, the ball so stop'd must be played where it lyes." Here, clearly, is a statement that makes the game what it is, for it tells us that we play golf outdoors, where others may intervene, and that luck, or the rub of the green as it's come to be known, is part of the game. The idea is brilliant in its simplicity. "Don't touch the ball," it says. "Play it as it is, wherever it is."

The rules eventually became more complex. Golf is indeed played on open ground, which means that unusual situations arise. But golfers who follow the essential principle of placing their ball on the tee and not touching it until they have holed out won't go far wrong.

That essential principle has been preserved in Britain as nowhere else in the golf world. Many courses haven't been changed in years, because the idea of playing the game on land more natural than created persists. And if the holes remain unaltered, then it seems proper that the ball should not be moved or touched. What man has not created — the position where one's ball comes to rest, for instance — man should not alter. The idea is to get on with the game, wherever the game takes you. And so, should your ball come to rest on the beach to the right of the last hole at the Waterville links in southwest Ireland, you play it from there. The seashore is part of the golf course. Should your ball land on the road behind the seventeenth green at the Old Course you play it from there, even though the shot isn't to be found in instructional textbooks. Playing the ball as it lies also ensures clean golf; there's no opportunity for controversy over whether one's opponent has taken unfair advantage; no "pick and kick" golf, as Helen McDonnell, a fine player and the daughter of British golf writer Michael McDonnell, points out.

The Old Course is golf's Mecca, as unadorned as a course can be, renowned for its lack of artifice and mysterious for the same reason. Here sits a narrow strip of treeless, featureless plain, barely 100 yards wide from side to side. Bleak is the word. Sam Snead wondered what the fuss was all about when first he rounded the bend in the road to come upon what looked like a moonscape. He soon learned about the ragged rupture known as Hell Bunker that crosses the fourteenth fairway, and that the line from the tee that would set up a shot to avoid Hell Bunker was well to the right, into the Elysian Fields. He and all golfers who have visited the Old Course have learned to consider the wind and the placement of the pin, and that the straight line isn't always the best line. The best line into the fourteenth green may be from well left of the obvious line. The second shot on the par-five ought to be well left of Hell Bunker and short of Grave Bunker. It's a lasting charm of British golf that one must sometimes aim well left or right to set up the most favorable angle into the green. The way the land moves determines the way one wants one's shot to move.

Very little may be obvious in British golf. If you can't see the back of the green from your position in the fairway, for instance, land your ball short: There's probably a nasty dip in the fairway. I was playing with a low-handicap player from Maryland who refused to bounce the ball into the greens when first he played British courses. It took him five or six days and many dollars lost to his companions before he accepted the shots he had to play. It's not advisable to fly the ball into the hard British greens. British golf is not target golf, where one lands the ball beside the hole on heavily watered greens, sure it will stick as if it landed in a vat of molasses. British golf is often bounce-the-ball golf. It's a ground game as well as an aerial game. It's important to know when to play the ground and when to take the aerial route.

The customs of British golf appeal to me. I like the firm ground of the links, or seaside courses. The fairways scoot down alleys and valleys by the sea, greens are set in hollows or precipices, bunkers are hidden from view. I like the ancient courses such as Prestwick in Scotland and Hunstanton in England with their blind holes that remind us that every shot in golf is actually a blind shot, since we are looking at the ball rather than our target as we swing. Blind holes exaggerate the truth and thereby proclaim it. The 207-yard fourteenth hole at Hunstanton is blind, playing over a sand hill that is more like a partition between one aspect of golf and another. The green is hidden beyond; one must stand on the tee and imagine the ball sailing over the dividing barrier, then landing on the other side and rolling bumpety-bumpety across the folds in the open ground near the hole. The hole is an odd one, but it belongs in golf, a game played on odd, uneven surfaces. Yet Hunstanton members voted in 1987 to take the hole out in favor of something conventional. To their eternal credit, the members soon voted it back in. They wanted their golf to remain timeless.

What a pleasure it is to play such courses. There's hardly a water hazard to be seen, certainly few that have been created. Neither pond nor lake impede the ball's progress, and so there's hardly a forced carry on British courses. The ocean isn't far away on most links, but it's there as a backdrop, although it can come into direct play when the wind is strong. Its real influence is to affect one's thinking; North American golfers aren't accustomed to hitting 135-yard four-irons. The wind also converts long holes into short holes, short holes into monsters.

The wind and the bounces and the blind shots show that golf is not "fair." We must accept what nature has wrought. Golf was never meant to be a fair game. The wind can turn right round on many courses, making the nine holes out a test against the wind, and the nine holes in also against the wind. Golfers in a tournament who go out in the afternoon might find the opposite. The same course can play half a dozen shots harder in the morning than the afternoon. This is why par makes little or no sense at British courses. Consider the wind and the conditions and compute your own par.

I remember the time I played Royal St. George's in Sandwich, England. It's one of the courses on the British Open rota, the most difficult, some say. I played it from the championship tees, and par was only a word. It bore no relationship to the course I played. Par on the card read seventy, but I calculated it as seventy-four and a quarter.

There was nobody on the course the late fall day that I played Sandwich, as it's known. As always in Britain, I played quickly. The courses encourage fast play. The lack of water hazards helps. British golfers also tend to play match play rather than medal play. Fast play comes easily because there's no point to continuing a hole when you're out of it. Put the ball in your pocket and move on to the next hole.

This isn't to say that the British don't keep score over full rounds. They do, but it's usually on what are known as medal days. Clubs designate these days, when golfers mark their cards and play golf the American way — medal play or stroke play. But it's a sometime thing, and many British golfers would as soon avoid it. They know that slow play inevitably follows. Medal play was unheard of in golf until the late nineteenth century. It's now the main game in professional tournaments and at most amateur tournaments, especially in North America. But match play is golf as an outing — hit the ball and hit it again until you're out of the hole. It's the reason my good friend Archie Baird can play four rounds over four different courses in one day once a year. He and three friends play his beloved Gullane #1 course east of Edinburgh, and three other courses in the area. "And we have time for lunch, a shower after our day's golf, and then dinner with our wives," Baird says. Baird's wife, Sheila, is a descendant of Willie Park, the first British Open champion. And Baird runs a golf museum in an old hut beside the first tee at Gullane #1.

This atmosphere makes you want to play well at British courses. I invariably play my best golf there, as do many others. Prior to the 1984 British Open at St. Andrews I visited Gullane, where I picked up a game with U.S. PGA Tour commissioner Deane Beman. Beman is a former tour player who had won the United States and British Amateurs. He loves to compete, and he defeated me one-up. We both played well, and I'm sure we were inspired by the setting. Who wants to lose on a splendid old links? Who wants to lose in an area where when you look around all you can see are golf courses? There's even a children's course across the road from Gullane #1.

Match play isn't the only form of golf that makes British golf such a delight. There's also alternate shots or, more properly, four-somes, in the original meaning of the term — four golfers playing alternate shots in teams of two, therefore only two balls in play. A letter posted in the Woking clubhouse in Surrey, England, tells the tale. Apparently a member had asked for four-ball privileges. The letter from the club secretary dated April 24, 1980, reads: "Woking has always been a two-ball club with a reputation for four-somes. It is not intended that this should change. There is a limited demand for four-ball games." The letter posts times when four-balls will be allowed: 10:30-12:00 and 2:30-3:00 on Saturdays and Sundays and bank holidays only. A notice at the West Sussex club in Pulborough points out that three- and four-ball games may be played only with the secretary's permission and must always give way to two-ball games, "irrespective of whether they are maintaining their position on the course."

Good for Woking and good for West Sussex. Foursomes is a lively and rare form of golf throughout most of the world and much missed by those who know its qualities. It's distressing to put one's partner in a deep sand pit after he's put you in an ideal position from the tee, and one plays foursomes in fear of such embarrassment. At the same time, the foursomes game is all about partnership, swallowing one's pride and playing on. It's a major part of the Ryder Cup matches and a source of widespread interest among British golfers, even if they grumble about it from time to time. It's hardly ever played in the United States or Canada. "In America," Henry Longhurst wrote, "anyone suggesting the playing of a Scotch foursome, as they call it, would render himself liable to be certified. In Britain every club golfer goes on record as saying that the foursome is the 'best form of golf,' while at the same time going to great pains to avoid playing one. Nevertheless, when the occasion is right, I very much doubt whether there *is* anything to beat a foursome."

I've played foursomes matches in which I wanted to scream at my partner when he followed my long drive straight down the middle with a topped shot into a bunker. I've also looked for an escape route after he hit an approach shot into the green within a few feet of the hole that I followed by missing the putt. But I still enjoy foursomes golf. A special camaraderie develops between the two golfers. We're connected by the golf ball that we share. Its fate lies in our mutual hands. Foursomes golf has a place in the game. That it's still part of British golf shows that the game is different there. The differences are worth maintaining.

Customs such as foursomes golf appear eccentric to first-time visitors, but soon seem quite right. Walking the course is another British custom, ridiculous as that sounds. Who would think that walking a course is even worth mentioning? Isn't golf all about walking? No longer, I fear. Many North American resort courses have effectively legislated against walking by forcing golfers to take golf carts. Directors of some private courses have discussed forcing golfers to ride carts at certain times. And a new English golf complex — note those words, *golf complex*, meaning courses, hotels, fancy dining rooms, hot tubs, etc., etc. — is taking shape south of London. It's the American concept, complete with a fleet of golf carts and fancy prices for membership. The complex will surely be beautiful, but it won't be British golf.

British golf is golf at such courses as Woking. Golfers here are still walking. Nor is riding the thing to do at West Sussex, where there is one buggy for hire, but only for members on a medically approved list. Applicants must provide a medical certificate to the secretary. Walking is part of the game in Britain, and well it should be. No doubt that will change as golf in Britain becomes more Americanized, but for now, walking is still encouraged. British golf is delightful in other ways that recall an earlier era.

Golf courses were part of the landscape, and often the center of recreation; so it follows that one can take a train, say, to the stop called Freshfield, walk off with a bag of clubs on one's shoulder, and emerge almost inside the professional's shop at Formby Golf Club. I took the train there one early morning during the 1983 British Open up the road at Royal Birkdale, in Southport, England, and was told to be careful not to depart the train at the stop marked Formby. It was Freshfield that would get me to the Formby course. It was as if the Winged Foot Golf Club, a United States Open course, were next door to Manhattan's Grand Central Station.

Henry Longhurst called the kind of golf I am describing "golf by train." He writes of a time when, "before it became a wartime casualty, Bramshot was a great 'train course' and several of us used to go there by train in preference to car." My encounters while taking the train to golf courses demonstrated how much a part of British life golf is; not that you can walk on to many courses directly from a train, but one doesn't feel out of place boarding a train with golf clubs in hand. More often than not one will make a friend and perhaps arrange a game.

But a golf course in Britain is often more than a golf course. It's also a park; it's countryside. Non-golfers walk the courses, a consequence of the old British custom of having established rights-of-way for the public on private property. So families stroll the Old Course in St. Andrews, taking exercise and air, as the British say, most evenings. Families of golfers walk and play; one early evening at Dooks in Ireland, a mother played the course with her husband, daughter, and son. They played out of two sets of clubs, walking their dog as they golfed. Another time I noticed four golfers on the Bruntsfield Links in Edinburgh; there was something more than vaguely similar about them. It turned out that they were four generations of one family: father, son, grandson, and great-grandson. And one afternoon I saw a woman riding her horse along a bridle path through the Walton Heath Golf Club in Surrey, England. "It's nice to get everybody together instead of sectioning them off," my companion for the day, Neil Heron, the club secretary's son, told me. People also walk their dogs, as do many golfers. Michael McDonnell says, "If you don't have a dog at Worplesdon (a course in Surrey), it's reckoned you're improperly dressed."

I played one match at Rye, a breezy, ancient, and bumpy golf course in Sussex, beside the English Channel. My companion was Hugh Blenkin, who was in charge of operations for the southeast area of the London police force. He was accompanied by his Labrador dog, Tessa, and all during the round he rhapsodized about his beloved Rye: "To come down here after a week in London, just to breathe the air, have a round. . . . We have some lovely members, and you can get a good lunch. . . . I do enjoy it here." No doubt he did, but Blenkin exploded after hitting a poor shot at a critical juncture in our match. "Oh, you pudding," he chastised himself after he dug up a divot as thick as a New York cut steak. Then he went on his way, briskly. A few minutes later he was in the clubhouse, dressed for lunch in jacket and tie.

Jacket and tie? Of course. They're mandatory in most clubhouse bars and dining rooms in Great Britain. I thought this was rather stuffy until I entered into the spirit. There are clothes for golfing, and there are clothes for drinking and dining. Besides, golfers wore uniforms hundreds of years ago, mostly red coats at first, then various colors for club jackets. They wore the jackets while playing; now jackets are worn at dinner. The custom helps make British golf the occasion that it is. I don't think I've ever enjoyed golf meals as much as when visiting British clubs. A pint of Guinness or a ginger beer, and soup and toasted cheese sandwiches — that's all I need. After I pay for the pint, the gentleman behind the bar says, "Thank you, kind sir." I've also heard "lovely," and "Thank you, dear," and "Of course, why not?" while sitting alone in a club room and asking if I could stretch out at a table for four.

These customs are all part of the warmth at the heart of authentic, British golf. But some well-known clubs such as Turnberry are starting to treat visitors less kindly. They advertise their courses as British Open championship layouts and then insist that golfers play off tees so far forward that they are playing a different course. I still enjoy playing these courses, although I don't like to see the insincerity implicit in the clubs' attitudes. My main objective in visiting Britain, however, has always been to play the lesser known courses. That's where I find authentic golf.

At Walton Heath, for instance, there is an artisans' club that consists of 140 people from the community. They pay a smaller membership fee than regular members, in return for which they help maintain the course. En masse they're out on the course some evenings, repairing divots, cleaning the course, painting the clubhouse. They have their own clubhouse and pub. One artisan is a millionaire who lives near the club. "They are essential," the club secretary, Sandy Heron, told me. "I don't know how clubs get along without them."

Many clubs also use caddies. They are particularly important on the flat, featureless links. Perplexed about how to line up a shot, or how far to hit it? Consult your caddie. "On that steeple in the town," he might suggest for the line of a drive. Or, "Corner of the clubhouse is the spot you're after, sir."

I usually hire a caddie when I play British courses. They help navigate me around the course and also add to the pleasure.

At the Portmarnock club near Dublin, Ireland, I hooked up with brothers Kevin and George Christie. George, fifteen, caddied for me in my first round. Kevin, eleven, caddied for me in the second, the same day. Neither was much taller than my golf bag. "Lashing about," as they said while running all over the course to follow some errant shots, they helped me play in no time at all. On the eighth, a 365-yard par-four, George suggested I aim my drive for the three chimneys in the distance. The line seemed far off what

I would have thought, but George was right. I would have hit the rough had I taken the direct line for the green. Coming home, Kevin Christie said it all.

"Home sweet home," he said as we approached the last green. "Will ye come back again? I hope ye will."

I assured Kevin I would, and I have. British golf generates a feeling of community. This spirit is very much a part of the game. Clubs accept societies of golfers, that is, groups that have some reason for getting together and whose members meet on courses, usually in one-day meetings. After the golf, they change clothes, have dinner, and pull out their diaries or calendars from their breast pockets to pencil in the next meeting.

Society golf is a most convivial way of competing and socializing. Simon White belongs to the 72 Club, a group of London-area men in their thirties who play a tournament each April at the Littlestone course in Kent. They play the seventy-two holes in one day, beginning at dawn and finishing at dusk, going out in two-balls, of course. White, a member at the West Surrey Club, has won the event. He's so fond of the Littlestone area that he and his wife and young son come down each fall for a weekend holiday. He doesn't play golf then, but he'll talk golf.

I met Simon an hour or so after I arrived at a hotel near Littlestone. I didn't know anybody, and so I headed for the lounge. Three hours and many brandies later, at 2:00 A.M., Simon and I said good-night and arranged to meet for golf a week or so later near his hometown of Guildford. Meanwhile, I played Littlestone, where I was introduced to an ideal drink for a cool autumn day — a whiskey mac, ginger wine with whiskey.

Simon, like all British golfers, enjoys a wager or two on his golf. But the wagering is small; it adds spice to the game, but the game is still the main thing. I haven't been to many British courses where golfers play for very much at all, no matter how wealthy they are. At the same time, British clubhouses sometimes seem designed so that members can wager on golfers coming up the final hole. The windows of the main lounge at Royal Troon are only a few feet behind the last green. I found it both humorous and unsettling to stand over a chip shot to the green while gentlemen in jackets and ties placed bets as to whether I could get down in two.

But this is British golf. It's a reminder of earlier times, a ramble and a wander beside the sea, across ancient footpaths, over heathland and across cliffside holes, toward the town as one plays the inward nine. Bernard Darwin once referred to the "extraordinary solitude that surrounds the individual player," when he golfed at Royal St. George's. I have found that solitude all over the British Isles and have also found companionship. There is a stillness about British golf, a silence and timelessness. Some people dream of Florida in the winter. I think of Ballybunion in late autumn, with a howling wind off the Atlantic Ocean and the eerie silence in the fairways bracketed by colossal dunes. British golf is both civilized and untamed, the game as it's meant to be played.

# SEVEN

# Moe Norman:
## Golf's Eccentric Genius

Golf-watching at tournaments is an agreeable and enlightening way of passing a few hours. The game's lack of precisely defined playing territory means that the spectator can observe a golfer at close range. The playing areas — at least the expected playing areas — may be roped off in modern tournaments, but the spectator can still examine the golfer in detail. Jack Nicklaus might hit his shot ten yards off the fairway, for instance, and find himself in the midst of a crowd, so much so that officials might have to ask the spectators to move back. A fan may also inadvertently affect play when he gets in the way of a golf ball. It's considered a rub of the green when a ball ricochets off a fan and back into the fairway. That's the happy side of the story. But a golfer might also hit a spectator and then find his ball in a bad lie in the rough. It's all part of the game.

There are no boards in golf as in hockey, no real grandstands as in baseball or football or tennis, notwithstanding the areas reserved for seating around greens at many events. The golf fan can seat himself beside a green all day long, as visitors to the Masters at the Augusta National Golf Club do; many set up their chairs in favorite spots hours before golfers will arrive, the better to get a close-up view. The golf fan may also walk with a particular group all the way round, thereby gaining a sense of the ebb and flow of his play. Or he may move from group to group, player to player, as he tries to catch a sampling of the golf being played. Whatever his mode of observation, the golf-watcher can live the game as the pros live it. He can watch as a golfer chats with his caddie, fiddles with his grip, and winces or smiles after he's hit a shot.

I've watched plenty of golf and plenty of golfers. A few players have so captured my imagination that I would travel great distances to watch them. My short list of current golfers would include Arnold Palmer, Jack Nicklaus, Lee Trevino, Tom Watson, Curtis Strange, Greg Norman, Seve Ballesteros, and Moe Norman. All but Moe Norman are famous players who have won major championships. I enjoy watching them because of their flair and precision, but also because they take pleasure in each shot. They are creative and involved. Every shot is a game in itself. They all want to score as low as possible, but more than that, they thrive on the act of striking the golf ball. Moe Norman, or simply Moe, as he is known to golfers around the world, shares these qualities, but he has never shown them to the golf world at large. I have gotten to know him, though, and find him the game's most fascinating player.

Palmer attacks every shot with gusto, as does Greg Norman. Nicklaus bends the golf course to his will with a concentration so formidable his wife, Barbara, often calls him Stonewall because he doesn't hear her if he's involved in something else. Trevino sets up well left of his intended target and then swivels his body round to produce shots that fly low and true. I also like watching him because of his ability to joke with his playing companions and the crowd almost until the second he hits the ball. Watson and Strange swing with technical precision, and neither makes excuses for a mistake. Ballesteros is a shot-making genius who can feel a wide repertoire of shots and then shape his body in such a way as to bring them off. I also enjoyed watching George Knudson. He could do anything he wanted with a golf ball. Nicklaus once said he had a million-dollar swing.

Then there's Moe Norman, the Canadian professional who dazzles anybody who watches him. Watson was once waiting to hit a tee shot in a PGA Tour event when the conversation around the tee turned to the question of who were the pure swingers in the game. Watson wheeled round. "Hey, I'll tell you about a guy who can hit it better than anybody. His name is Moe Norman, up in Canada."

Trevino speaks with particular sensitivity about Norman. "I don't know of any person that I've ever seen," Trevino told his interviewer on a documentary about Norman for the Canadian Broadcasting Corporation, "who could strike a golf ball like Moe Norman as far as hitting it solid, knowing where it's going, knowing the mechanics of the game, and knowing what he wanted to do with the golf ball. When you're talking about Moe Norman you're talking about a legend, and I'm talking about a living legend because the public doesn't know Moe Norman. Ask any golf professional, whether you're in Australia, the U.S. or Great Britain, and they say that's the Canadian guy that hits it so damn good, isn't it, and I say that's him. He's a legend with the professionals. The guy's a genius when it comes to playing the game of golf."

Norman, who was born in 1929, uses an original style that appears to invent a new language of the game. He's an enigma. Talent such as his deserves center stage, but Moe has spent his life far from the golf world's spotlight. Still, there's no denying his talent. He's a prodigy.

Is golf cerebral? Norman has mastered it with instinct and imagination. Must technique conform to strict principles? Norman's method seems to defy convention while causing observers to wonder what's going on and to speculate about what makes his swing send the ball off so cleanly nearly every time. Is golf slow, a labored enterprise where the player has too much time to think? Norman plays it with the speed of a gazelle. He takes one look at his target and he swings. For him, this flick-of-a-switch speed neutralizes golf's psychological complexities. Most golfers take between ten and twenty seconds from address to swing completion. He takes three seconds. Norman calls himself "the 747 of golf. One look at the target and I'm gone. Miss 'em quick. That's always been my theme song." Officials at a tournament once asked him to zigzag his way down the fairways rather than walking straight down the middle; he was playing so quickly that they needed to slow him down.

Norman makes golf look as easy as tossing a coin. Whereas most golfers arrange themselves loosely over the ball before swinging, Norman appears rigid. He stands far from the ball, his arms stretched to the limit, his feet far apart in a wide stance. He places the clubhead a foot or so behind the ball rather than directly behind it. This simple, casually brilliant maneuver enables Norman to follow the golf dictum that one should take the club back from the ball long and low, combing the ground along the way. He's a foot back before he starts, and then swings his club straight back from the ball and through it, extending his arms and club farther, perhaps, than any golfer in the history of the game. His extension through the ball protects the clubhead from fluttering and accounts in part for his uncanny accuracy. He demonstrates his clubhead extension by putting a silver dollar on the ground thirty-seven inches behind the ball. The sole plate of his driver contacts the coin every time. Then he moves the coin twenty-two inches ahead of the ball and contacts it again every time. Every shot is straight, every swing a carbon copy of the one that came before. He's so accurate that he's worn a dark spot the size of a quarter in the middle of all his iron clubs.

There was the time Norman gave a clinic during a Canadian Professional Golfers' Association Seniors Championship in Winnipeg. He hit the flag three times. Another day, Norman was having breakfast in New Smyrna Beach, Florida, when fellow pro Ken Duggan asked him why he wasn't playing. "I hit the flagpole the first three holes," Norman said. "Why go on? Can't do any better than that." He shot sixty-nine during a Senior PGA Tour event in Vancouver while playing with Australian Ken Nagle; at four-under par through eleven holes, he then became upset on the twelfth hole when his shot spun back off the green into rough. "It's one of the most amazing exhibitions of ball-striking I've ever seen," Nagle said after the round. "If he hadn't let that incident bug him, he would have shot sixty-three or sixty-four. But he kept repeating what had happened. He couldn't drop it."

Some years ago I wandered into the pro shop at the Pinehurst #2 course in North Carolina. A fellow in the shop told me that Norman had just come through Pinehurst the week before on his way home from Florida, where he spends his winters, living cheaply.

"See the 'A' in Advantage?" the fellow asked, pointing to a canvas backing hung fifteen feet from where a golfer would hit balls in the indoor teaching area for the Advantage Golf School. The word was printed on the canvas. "Well, Moe Norman came in here last week and hit the bottom part of the 'A' five times in a row." That's nothing. Another time, he showed up at the Tomoka Oaks course in Daytona Beach to play four holes prior to a tournament. Up at 6:00 A.M., he was on the course at seven, hitting six balls from the tee. His friend, professional Ken Venning, showed up soon after and saw that three balls were touching. "Am I seeing mushrooms?" Venning asked Norman. "Or are those the shots you hit?" They were indeed Norman's shots; the three other balls were nearby.

"If they had a tournament in the dark," Norman says, "I'd be the only one who could play. I'd know where to walk." He can still recall the exact yardages and configurations of golf holes he hasn't seen in years. I sat at a table once as he rhymed off the lengths and patterns of the holes at the Royal Birkdale Golf Club in Southport, England. He hadn't played the course in twenty years. As a boy he played at the public Rockway club near Kitchener, Ontario, seventy miles west of Toronto. Norman and his pals often went out in a gangsome. The large group didn't keep score, not formally anyway. But after the round, Norman would remember every golfer's score on each hole.

Sometimes it seems every golfer has a Moe Norman story. Paul Azinger, the fine PGA Tour golfer, was astonished when he first came across Norman. Azinger was then a freshman at Brevard Junior College in Florida and was hitting balls with his teammates when his teacher, John Redman, told them to stop. "Boys," Redman said, "here comes the best ball-striker that ever lived."

"I couldn't believe what I was seeing," Azinger told me. "I've hit balls for a couple of hours, it's a hundred degrees, and here comes this guy in a long-sleeve turtleneck. I watched him hit drivers at the two-hundred-and-fifty-yard sign, and he never hit one more than ten yards left or right of the marker.''

Azinger makes a habit of watching Norman whenever he can. He and other golfers gather most years during the Canadian Open as Norman gives an impromptu clinic in his street shoes, using somebody else's clubs. Norman once gave a private demonstration for Ben Crenshaw. Crenshaw learned why Norman's nickname is Pipeline Moe. Moe never thinks of obstacles on the golf course. ''They're not in my jurisdiction,'' he explains, ''not in my vocabulary.''

Norman's skills have brought him some fifty pro tournament victories. He holds thirty-three course records. He turned fifty in 1979 and won the next seven Canadian Professional Golfers' Association senior championships. Yet he has never succeeded on the U.S. PGA Tour and refuses to try to qualify for the rich Senior PGA Tour. His prowess with a golf club begs the question: Why hasn't he succeeded on the world's tours? Why isn't his name all over the record books?

The answer lies in Norman's personality. He suffers from an inferiority complex so pervasive that it's kept him out of the mainstream of golf. George Knudson once said in a dinner line that Norman was second to none in ball-striking. He didn't know that Norman was behind him; Norman started to cry, so much respect did he have for Knudson's opinion, so little belief in himself. ''He is,'' Knudson said, ''the most sensitive man I know.''

After winning the 1955 Canadian Amateur in Calgary, Alberta, Norman hid beside the Elbow River rather than speak at the presentation. After he won the 1956 Canadian Amateur in Edmundston, New Brunswick, Canadian sportswriter Hilles Pickens described him as ''a strange, highly gifted fellow who hit the ball with such supreme indifference to normal graces yet almost made a travesty of its well-known difficulty.''

In 1958, having turned professional the year before and having played one winter on the U.S. Tour, Norman declared that he'd had enough. ''I didn't feel at home there. I always felt they were superior to me, that they were gods, that I was their servant. All of a sudden I'm talking to the best in the world. I had no money, they got money. I'm trying to make enough to go to the next tournament, they're leaving five-dollar tips." Norman's refusal to compete at the game's highest levels is golf's loss as much as it may have been his. Peter Dobereiner claimed in the *Observer* in 1984 that Norman is the greatest of the golfers he knows who deliberately chose not to become champions.

Norman lived much of his adult life north of Toronto in a room without a phone, picking up his messages at a driving range nearby. Then he moved near Kitchener, west of Toronto, living in a motel room, also without a phone. His friend Nick Weslock, long one of the game's top amateurs, says that the phone is like a cobra to Norman. He'd rather not touch it. His real home is his car — the trunk is filled with a dozen pairs of golf shoes, 300 practice golf balls, an assortment of clubs. Clothes take up the back seat, and his books, scraps of paper, tapes, and notes for speeches are spread over the front seat. A shirt and a sports jacket can usually be found on a hanger. He often sits for a few hours at the side of a country road and studies his books. When he eats, it's usually in a fast-food restaurant. He's as elusive as a hole in one, wandering from course to course. Each spring, though, he can be found at the Brantford Golf and Country Club, southwest of Toronto, where he packs his big golf bag full of golf balls and walks nine holes alone, carrying his own bag.

Norman amazes observers. I caddied in the same group in which he played during the third round of the 1981 Canadian Professional Golfers' Association championship at Kitchener's Westmount Golf and Country Club. Norman bounced a ball on the head of his driver as he arrived at the first tee just a minute or so before his starting time. Many spectators didn't see his shot because he was so fast. The ball flew long and straight down the fairway.

Most of the people there wouldn't have noticed the shot even if they paid close attention because they were too busy laughing. Nobody knew what to make of Moe. "See, that's how it's been all my life," Norman said while walking down the fairway. "Other players hit good shots and the crowd cheers. I hit a good shot and they laugh. All my life. For years I've been Canada's laughing stock

in golf. If anybody's been through it, I have. But I'm not bitter
if that's the way life is. I'm just a different type of golfer, fastest
player in the world, take one look and whack. It doesn't look like
I'm trying.''

Professional golf involves more than hitting the ball. There are
travel arrangements to be made, interviews and social obligations,
standards of dress and conduct to be considered. Norman has not
been able to deal with this side of the game. Maybe he needed a
manager, somebody at his side all the time. That's a common opinion, but it may not be a practical solution.

''I think that if someone would have taken Moe under his wing,''
Lee Trevino points out, ''and had said, 'Look, we're going to play
here, and don't be afraid of the questions that you're going to be
asked, I'm going to tell you what to say' — well, I think that Moe
just didn't want to deal with the media and with the public. Moe
wanted to play golf and he wanted to win tournaments. He's a very
shy person — that's the one thing you have to remember about Moe
Norman. He doesn't like to be around a lot of people. He likes
to be around his friends and when you play golf and you play in-
ternationally, you're going to meet a lot of people who will try to
take advantage of you and ask some questions that maybe you don't
want to answer. I don't think Moe ever wanted to be in that
situation.''

Paradoxically, Norman's overwhelming insecurity may be the
source of his remarkable talent. I've come to believe in the twenty-
five years that I've watched and gotten to know him that without
his desire to get out of everyone's way, he might not be so speeded
up. Without the speeding up that is the essential component of his
golfing personality, he might have tried a more conventional way
of hitting the ball. There may then have been no offbeat setup, no
pure, instinctive swing, no mechanical precision. It's possible that
his vulnerability — his shadow — has produced behavior that meshes
exactly with the demands of the game itself but renders him unable
to cope with the social and business part. I think that he knew
without saying so that to try to adapt to the golf world would have
meant the loss of his distinctive way of playing. Moe Norman likes
hitting the golf ball too much to ever have considered such a sea

change. Besides, Norman on the course moves to his own accelerated rhythm. He cannot be curbed, tamed, or slowed down.

I first encountered Norman in the early 1960s at the De Haviland Golf Centre in Toronto, where he worked as an assistant pro. His job was to entertain patrons with his maximum-efficiency swing. I was just a boy, but news of Norman's exploits traveled far down the golfing line. Night after night he arrived at De Haviland to put on his show. There was a two-tiered driving range where one could hit balls off rubber tees placed on rubber mats; there was also a substantial practice putting green, a nine-hole course, and an eighteen-hole par-three course that was floodlit for night play. My routine became a ritual. I'd buy a pail of balls in the small shop, walk onto the lower driving line, and head over to Norman. He was always in the middle of the line, smashing balls into the night. "High fade, you want a high fade?" he'd repeat in his characteristic rapid-fire speech. And then he'd hit it, exactly as was called for. The ball was on a string. Norman made the vast practice field his own, and if you happened to be a youngster beginning golf, as I was, he would give you all the time you wanted. He loves children. He is in many ways a child himself, a prodigy who was never meant for an adult world that he perceived as hostile.

Moe was unforgettable. He seemed a sorcerer come to the night to demonstrate what golf was all about. It wasn't about winning money or becoming a head professional at a fancy country club. It wasn't even about entering tournaments, or winning the Masters. It was about playing. It was about joy. It was a simple game best played in an almost naive way. He rang with delight while hitting balls.

"*Let* your body enjoy the shot," Moe would tell the crowd. "*Let* it enjoy the shot. That's the biggest word in golf, *let*." And then he might define the game. "Golf," he said. "It's hitting an object to a defined target area with the least amount of effort and an alert attitude of indifference." Don't care so much about results, then. That's what I heard. Swing the club. Forget about the shot when it's over. Looking back on those days at De Haviland, I know what attracted me to Norman. It was the happiness he exuded when he stood over and hit the ball. It's the same quality I've seen since to varying degrees in other golfers. But it was and still is the main component of Moe's game.

Norman became a source of wonder to me. I watched him hit balls at De Haviland and then walked to the par-three course with a seven-iron, wedge and putter, just to see if it were possible to enjoy the game when there were real targets. The memory of having just watched Moe, along with the separate world here — floodlights illuminating the course, the white of the golf ball soaring through the blackness — helped me wriggle into the game's core. Flashes of steel broke the darkness as golf shafts flickered across the course. I felt on stage, alone, given the gift of golf at night by a man who wanted to remain anonymous, but whose style and substance would render that impossible.

I continued to watch Moe whenever I could. Gradually I got to know him — as much as that's possible — and in 1983 spent the better part of a week chatting with him at a Senior PGA Tour event in Calgary. He was at home here in the city where he'd won his 1955 Canadian Amateur and where he gained further recognition by winning the 1966 Canadian Professional Golfers' Association championship. What did it matter that he stayed at the low-rent Flamingo Hotel while Arnold Palmer and Bob Goalby stayed at a fancy hotel, or that he stopped at fast-food places while they frequented fine restaurants? They dined. He ate. One evening we ate at McDonald's, and as a six-year-old boy cavorted on the counter, Moe asked, "See that boy? He's enjoying himself. Know why? Because he doesn't know where he is, because he doesn't know where he is."

This was more than twenty years after I'd run across Moe. The child in him was still prominent. It defined him. And yet its strong presence raised the question of why he was the way he was. There was a mystery about him, and I wanted to learn more.

Moe and his twin sister, Marie, were the second- and third-born of six children. Their father worked for a furniture company in Kitchener and, although the family was hardly well off, they lived comfortably. Murray — his original given name — was five years old when he suffered a head injury when he was hit by a car while sleigh-riding. He was dragged a hundred yards, but ran home apparently unhurt. The accident may have led to his rapid speech and movement; his mother always regretted that he wasn't examined for possible injury, but without neuropsychological testing it's impossible to know what, if any, were the effects of the accident.

As a schoolboy, Norman was more interested in sports than studies. He hit .610 in a softball league, where he was known as a singles hitter who could place the ball wherever he wanted. In school, meanwhile, he liked math and could rattle off the answers to multiplication questions without thinking. Marie Kelly, his twin, remembers him as a high-strung youngster, quick to retreat into himself if crossed. He was physical, too, jumping thirty feet from a bridge into a snowbank, or leaping to the ground from the highest branch of a willow tree.

Moe left school in the ninth grade. He was spending more time at the Rockway Golf Club than in class, having taken to the game that gives loners freedom of expression. The course became his home and professional Lloyd Tucker became his teacher. Tucker coached Moe without trying to alter his style. The first time Moe stepped up to the ball was the first time he set up in his unique position. He never changed. Moe hit up to 800 balls a day right from the start, transforming his hands into a vise with the texture of sandpaper. Black callused ridges run along the fingers of his left hand like furrows in a field. "Scratch it all you want," he says, "it doesn't hurt." Nick Weslock claims Moe could put the hand through a pane of glass without tearing it up.

While competing as a young amateur, Moe hitchhiked to events and slept in sand traps or on benches. He set pins in a Kitchener bowling alley to earn a few dollars and became the fastest pin-boy around, a whirling dervish of the lanes. Wherever he went, he drew attention. Golf was his one love. "It became his life," Marie says. "He used to tell us that someday he would be the richest guy in the world because of golf."

He certainly seemed on his way, winning both the 1955 and 1956 Canadian Amateur championships. After his first win, he was greeted by a group of fellow golfers who led him back to the course in a small motorcade. Moe sat in the corner at what was to be a celebration, too shy to say a word. Yet even as he turned inward, golf was propelling him forward. He was invited to the 1956 Masters. "I was setting up pins one night when it was ten below," he remembers, still awestruck, "and when I got home, here's this invitation to the Masters. What a thrill."

Surrounded by thousands of fans, Norman trembled on the first tee at the Augusta National Golf Club. "I was shaking like a leaf. But before they could say 'Moe Norman,' bang, I hit it down the middle." He conquered fear with speed, but he didn't complete the Masters. After the first round, Sam Snead gave him a lesson that so excited him that he hit 800 balls that evening. But by taking the lesson at a critical time, he betrayed his fundamental problem: He didn't believe in his own ability to play against such competition.

Four hours later, as darkness fell over the range, his hands were raw. He could hardly grip the club the next day because he had split a thumb; he withdrew after nine holes of the second round. It's been said that he walked off because play was too slow, or because he felt uncomfortable. Irv Lightstone, a Toronto professional who was with him, says Norman was in too much pain to continue.

Later that year, Moe again won the Canadian Amateur, and the Royal Canadian Golf Association selected him to represent the country in a match against the United States and Mexico. But he was dropped only a few days before the team was to leave for Mexico. The RCGA had heard that Norman had been asked by Revenue Canada to pay taxes on money he had earned passing the hat at golf clinics; taking money for golf contravened the amateur code. Moe had also been criticised for selling prizes he won at tournaments, but he needed the money. He was rumored to have intentionally finished second or third in a tournament rather than first, so that he might win household goods that his mother could use. Moe admitted to passing the hat at golf clinics and proudly showed off the letter from the tax department. RCGA president Jim Anglin tried to reach Moe for an explanation. When he didn't reply, Anglin cut him from the team. "I took him off," Anglin says, "not because he had taken money, but because he hadn't communicated." Moe saw the incident as a sign that he didn't belong in the upper echelons of amateur golf.

He turned pro for the 1957 season and won money in his first tournament, an event to help fund Canadian pros under thirty. Unfortunately, the golf authorities — this time the Canadian Professional Golfers' Association — clobbered him again. He had no official status as a club pro, since he didn't work at a club, and was deemed ineligible to win money. He didn't get the $1,500 that was to support him for ten events on the United States winter tour. Moe was a winner with no money to show for his effort, seemingly neither pro nor amateur, in limbo. Toronto golf entrepreneur Bert Turcotte came to his rescue, hiring him at De Haviland, where I first saw him.

Moe did get to keep his winnings after placing in the next bursary event. He was in contention in the latter stages at one U.S. event, but then faltered. "I started trying a little too hard," he explains, "to bring a win back to Canada." But Moe had predicted his own decline. Asked to say why he had done so well as an amateur and to comment on his prospects as a pro, he answered, "I don't have anything to play for in amateur tournaments. If I turned pro and the bucks were on the line, I'm sure it would be a different story."

A different story indeed. Moe never felt comfortable in the United States. A pro told him that if he were going to play on the tour, he had better improve his grooming — his pants were often above his ankles, his toenails occasionally stuck through his shoes. And tour officials admonished him for his antics; he had hit balls off Coke bottles during the Los Angeles and New Orleans Opens. "I was putting on a show," he says, "making the crowd laugh. But they told me this was big business, this was *the* tour of the world, that they didn't care how good I was, I had to tee it up in the normal way."

After Moe played his ten United States events, he left the tour there for good, abandoning his childhood vision of getting rich from golf. He played the 1963 Canadian Open at the Scarboro Golf and Country Club, where Toronto Maple Leaf hockey star Teeder Kennedy told him that he could win. "I'm a teaching pro," Moe countered, "not a playing pro." Nevertheless, Moe played well enough to lie in second place after fifty-four holes, only three shots from the lead. But he started to think about what he would say if he won and became nervous. His agitation showed on the greens, where he three-putted six times. "I blew that tournament," he says. "Tee to green I was comfortable. Not on the greens. Shaky like a leaf. No self-confidence. I didn't know how to get the ball in the hole. The Canadian Open was controlling me. I wasn't controlling it. It was eating me because I wanted to win so bad." Moe hit the ball so well that it could make a person cry, but he was too frightened to compete. His form was immaculate, but he also embodied the golfing truth that errors in the swing often begin in the mind; his mind was shot through with fear.

Eventually, though, Moe felt more at ease around people. It took years, and the change was slow, but you could see it. Moe no longer gave a thought to playing in the United States. He entered fewer and fewer important Canadian events as he turned fifty. Instead, he studied books of popular psychology, and in spending more time with words and ideas, came to realize that others shared feelings he had. It was okay to live in relative solitude, to look for peace of mind, to express oneself in a particular way. You didn't have to belong to the world of golf at large. It was more important to belong to the world of golf you could create. Golf gave a person that chance.

In 1977 Moe met Irv Schloss and Paul Bertholy, teachers who emphasized the mental side of golf. He found that he could incorporate into other areas of life their ideas of how attitude affects performance on the golf course. Now he can speak after dinner at pro-ams. He can enjoy himself on the course with people he has only just met. "I couldn't mix with people when I was younger," Moe says. "I couldn't mix words. I couldn't go to dinner, sit down with people. They'd come up with these big words that I couldn't understand. And I didn't think it was important to mix with them. I knew I was never going to be an alderman or a mayor of a city. All I wanted was to become the straightest hitter the world has known and to get that goddamn ball in the hole."

I played a round of golf with Moe at the Maple Downs course,

north of Toronto. We were joined by Norman Mogil, the 1962 Canadian Junior champion who is a student of the game. He'd watched
Moe for years and touched on some significant themes.

"Moe is a man without guile," Mogil said, "and the world is
full of people with guile. It's very sad. The world has made a buf-
foon out of him. Society doesn't tolerate extreme behavior. The
irony is that he chose or ended up in a game where his behavior
would be so apparent. Obviously he could only play an individual
game, but it would be easier on him in a team game. He wouldn't
be as visible. Or maybe he should have been a football player or
a boxer, where he could expend a high level of energy all the time."

The physical gestures to which Mogil referred and which Norman
showed as a boy are still apparent. He walks up to a friend and
feigns a shoulder block. Once he picked up pro Gary Slatter and
turned him head over heels to see if he had any money in his pockets.
He used to pinch another golfer on the face so hard that the fellow
had to tell him to stop. Moe was just being affectionate, but he
doesn't know his own strength.

As he turned sixty, Moe was spending most of his time alone or
on the course. That hadn't changed. Every night in bed, he
memorizes a few pages from one of his self-help books and reminds
himself that somewhere that day people were talking about him.
PGA Tour player Peter Jacobsen has said that Moe is the most
talked-about golfer off the course because he plays the game so
exotically well.

The golf that Moe played at Maple Downs was typical. He shot
an error-free seventy. On one narrow hole he used a driver; his playing partners used irons to ensure they'd keep the ball in the fairway and out of the trees. His shot went so straight you could have
used it as the centerpiece in a mathematical theorem. Here was proof
that the shortest distance between two points is indeed a straight
line. Moe hit the shot, then reminded us of his credo: "So what
if the fairway is just thirty yards wide? The ball fits the Moe Norman way, the ball fits the Moe Norman way."

Moe hit another shot that was particularly arresting. He had
driven just off the fairway on the par-five first hole and into deep
rough. I would have taken a mid-iron to return the ball to the

fairway. And I probably would have gripped the club hard, the better, I might have figured, to get it through the thick rough. But Moe did it differently. He gripped the club so lightly he could have been holding a butterfly. His long, languid swing gained him unforced access to the path toward the ball. The ball popped out of the rough and flew for the green. "You have to use smooth centrifugal force in this game," Moe advised after the shot. "Everybody uses brute force, not smooth force. I swung way easier on that shot. Everybody else swings harder."

As beautifully as Moe played, he also displayed the flaws that have kept him apart. On that same hole where he used a driver while the rest of us used irons, he found his tee ball resting in a cut of rough just short of the green. He'd hit the ball perfectly into the middle of what he thought was fairway, but it finished in the rough. The seeming unfairness of it all bothered him. "What's this? What's this? Hit the ball perfect and I'm in the rough. That's not golf." Moe dwelled on the point until he got over the ball. He had trouble accepting that a golf course is a piece of land, and that designers and course superintendents can influence the game by changing the texture of the playing surface.

Moe also has trouble when he can't see the target. His mind works best when he sees the problem directly in front of him. Here's the ball. There's the flag. They become associated in his mind's eye, and the connection triggers his swing. It's as if he gets a strong visual impression that he must act on immediately lest he lose the image. He has difficulty, then, when he faces a blind shot, as he did on Maple Downs' seventh hole. His approach shot had to carry a hill that impeded his view of the green. Moe seemed unsettled over the ball, lost, without cues to swing. He didn't know where to go and couldn't manufacture an image long enough for it to have an effect. And so he swung inconclusively. The ball flew off line.

On the greens, meanwhile, Moe was insecure. He's at his best when hitting the ball. But the green is a stage upon which a private person might feel ill at ease. It's the most public part of a course; there's no place to get away or to hide. It's also difficult to discern exactly what constitutes a proper stroke. Putting is as much an art as a science.

Moe knows this, and so he doesn't enjoy putting. Neither did Ben Hogan or George Knudson. Ball-striking interested them, not putting. Moe kept saying during our round at Maple Downs that he and Knudson got so much pleasure out of swinging because they were always aiming at a definite target. The flight of the ball in the air wasn't affected by imperfections in the grass, as it may have been on the greens. Besides, they could understand the mechanics of the full swing. The putting stroke is so short that there's little room for analysis. It's more a matter of feel.

I rarely saw Moe on the practice putting green. Why put in time when you don't know what to work on? His putting reflects his uncertainty. He seems uninvolved. His hands waver. The stroke isn't decisive. And he listens to anybody, thereby betraying his insecurity. All golfers listen to tips to some degree, but it's unfortunate that a golfer who hits the ball so accurately tee to green has so little confidence in his abilities on the green. For the reality is that Moe exaggerates his problems on the green. His putting stroke is just fine, if only he would let it be. As soon as he misses a short putt, though, he's lost.

I've watched Moe putt for years and always thought his stroke was fluid enough. He accelerates the putter through the ball, one of the two or three fundamentals of putting. The ball rolls better than he thinks it does, even with his often indecisive stroke. I reminded him at Maple Downs of the good things I saw in his stroke. It surprised me that he seemed to be hearing this for the first time. When I told him that I thought he kept his right hand going toward the target, it was as if he had no idea that this was what he did, and that it worked. He couldn't stop talking about it the rest of the way. "That's what I do, is it? I didn't know that. I'll just do that the rest of the way, then, that's what I'll try to do."

But there's no changing Moe. I wouldn't try. Would you try to change Trevino or Ballesteros? Something would be lost. The way to be with Moe is just that, to simply be with him, to watch and marvel, and to respect him for his ball-striking ability. His very being raises questions about the game and about what it takes to play it well. Moe is unique. He's a reference point for anybody who thinks he hits the ball properly.

Is he a success? That's another question. It's a question that lingered on a fall evening in the glittering dining room at Kitchener's Westmount Club not that long ago, where Moe's fellow professionals were honoring him. He had started at Westmount as a ten-year-old caddie.

Moe had told me often that he was happy. "I did what I wanted to do. Being successful in this world is when you're doing something you love. I've done what I loved for thirty-five years, chase a golf ball. I gave Moe Norman a chance in this world to prove to the world what he has. I think I've proven it. I've got something people wanted, to hit the ball in a repetitive way. I can control my destiny from tee to green. I did it for thirty-five years and I'm still doing it. So how can I feel bad? Not when I got something everybody in the world wants. No sirree, I feel good, I feel good."

To me, Moe remains the golfer at De Haviland. He's hitting golf balls into the night sky while showing a youngster that the game can be a source of delight. I don't know if I understand him any better now than I did thirty years ago. But that doesn't matter. What matters is that Moe Norman is still hitting golf balls, still wandering from course to course, still enjoying the meeting of the club-face against the ball. He swings, and he lives. It's impossible to think of Moe Norman without golf.

Henry David Thoreau wrote that the highest of the arts is to "affect the quality of the day." Moe has done this for me every time I have watched him.

Lloyd Tucker, Moe's first and only teacher, the man who had the good sense not to try to change him, spoke at Westmount about his mysterious protégé. "If you've seen Fred Astaire," he said, "you've seen the best dancer; if you've seen Peggy Fleming, you've seen the best skater; and when you've seen Moe Norman hit a golf ball, you know you've seen the best that ever hit a golf ball." Moe sat quietly, but when he was praised time after time, he stood and waved to his friends.

# EIGHT

# Speaking of Golf:
# The Language of the Game

Most any golfer who has just played either the best or the worst round of his life can hardly wait to tell the nearest person the story of his success or failure. He wants the world to know how well he can play when he's really on his game, or conversely, to unburden himself of the ghastly misfortunes that befell him on his way to a horrible round. At times like this, the best thing his listener can do is to say, "Look, pal, it's not how, it's how many."

That's true as far as statistics go, but the bare number alone doesn't tell the story. Moe Norman's scores, for instance, often don't even begin to indicate his ball-striking talent. There are all kinds of ways to shoot any number, and too many boring ways to describe the rounds. I know as soon as I pick up the telephone and hear the voice of one particular fellow that I'm in for a monologue. He'll invariably tell me that he has to describe one shot he hit; but I know he won't stop. I cradle the phone between my shoulder and ear, then get to work sealing envelopes or bringing my checkbook up to date. Meanwhile, he goes on, a full eighteen holes' worth of how he played. If he's going to fill my ears with his exploits — the good, the bad, the ugly, the birdies, the bogeys, the out-of-bounds shots — doesn't he know that he could at least use more colorful language? Thankfully, the game has its own jargon. I just wish he used it. He could enliven the one-way conversation. "I wasn't leading and lagging," he might say about a poor game, à la Moe Norman. Or, again like Moe, "you need progression of power. I didn't have that today."

There was the day my friend shot seventy-seven, not very good for him, and a round I heard about almost before he had walked off the final green. I dread the day he brings a portable phone to the course. He'll be calling me immediately after he's eagled a hole. As for his seventy-seven, meanwhile, I would have been more in- terested had he called and said, "Lorne, you won't believe it. Sunset Strip for me today. And I covered the flag all day. Couple of quads on the rugs. Unbelievable." Now *that*'s better. At least he's vary- ing the pitch. "Sunset Strip." "Covered the flag." "Couple of quads on the rugs." I like it. The term "Sunset Strip" comes from the old American television show, "77 Sunset Strip." "Covered the flag" tells me that my friend was hitting his irons right at the flagstick all day. But he couldn't putt. Those "couple of quads on the rugs" indicate he four-putted two greens.

Now he's talking, and I can listen to him. When he shoots eighty — poor man — he can tell me he shot "Quebec par," a cruel reference to the idea that golfers from that province are not as accomplished as elsewhere, and that eighty is about as good as they can expect, par for the course, one might say. At least it's better than eighty-eight, also known as "piano keys" or "twin snowmen." Then there's a score of a hundred or more, "triple figures," as some misanthropic golfers call this all-too-common tally.

These expressions are part of a game that has always had a rich language and whose participants constantly invent new descriptions. Maybe it's not surprising; after all, the word "golf" itself is a derivative of the German word *kolbe*, according to Robert Brown- ing's *A History of Golf. Kolbe* also means club, and from it the French *chole* and the Dutch *kolf* or *colf* have derived. All are games played with a club, though some people argue that "golf" didn't derive from the German *kolbe* at all, but from the Dutch *het kolven*, a game played indoors over short distances using heavy clubs and large wooden balls. The Dutch golf historian Stephen van Hengel wrote in his book *Early Golf* (1972) that *het kolven* was itself a derivative of a game called *spel metten kolve*. He traced this form of Dutch golf back to 1296, when villagers who lived in Loenen, Holland, had a four-hole course. The game was played until 1830, according to van Hengel. Robert Price, a Welsh geographer and geologist who has studied the Scottish glacial landforms that gave rise to the courses there, points out in his book *Scotland's Golf Courses* that *colf* in Holland preceded golf in Scotland by at least a century. This leads me to think that the Dutch probably developed their own jargon of the game, now lost in antiquity. I wonder what score was represented by "Dutch par."

Historians have not had much success in using language to determine the game's origins. Browning called his chapter about the origins of golf "The Argument of Language," thereby emphasizing the debate. He wants no part of the position that the game began in Holland. The argument is still going on, and since I'm neither a lexicographer nor a philologist, I cannot contribute much to the debate here. But I'm not writing to learn the origins of the game according to language. I am not here to debate the merits of one argument versus another. I wish to celebrate golf's language, not to formalize it. Let the jargon flourish. Let us invent words and phrases. Let us express ourselves not only with our golf clubs. Golf is a silent enough game, so let us speak. I, for one, am pleased to hear something new. I reach for my notebook. I learn how often we respond to the game in a spontaneous, unpredictable way via an unsophisticated, non-technical language.

It's easy to see how some new phrase enters the vernacular, although it's not so simple to trace the mental processes that go into its formulation. A golfer begins his day on a place so apparently mundane that we call it, obviously, the driving range. He drives balls there, and it's a field, or a range, as in a shooting range. But before long he's trying to find his swing, and he's hitting hundreds of golf balls. The driving range is transformed into the "pound

ground.'' He's pounding balls in what is often a vain effort to come
up with something that will work, and he's still on a field, a ground.
But the other meaning could be that he's vainly pounding the
ground, or even pounding himself into the ground. How many of
us have put in our hopeful hours on the range only to emerge more
befuddled than when we began? What do you know? The driving
range that became the pound ground is now ''maniac hill.'' You're
in ''GUR'' territory (game under repair).

Eventually the golfer reaches the first tee. I use an iron from the
first tee at my course, since the fairway narrows in the area I might
reach with a driver; a stream to the right and woods and out of
bounds to the left convince me that prudence is the wise course.
An ''iron for accuracy,'' then, except when I don't hit it accurately.
Should I hook the ball, I can still hit it out of bounds, o.b., or
''Oscar Brown.'' That will necessitate my pulling another golf ball
out of the bag, a ''nugget,'' as the pros call it, or an ''autre pelota,''
which is what one golfer asked me for when I was caddying for him.

A golfer can choose from a wide variety of clubs when he's on
the tee. In golf's early days, he might have gone with a ''play club,''
the original term for a driver. Nowadays he can choose from a conventional wooden-headed driver, or a ''metalwood,'' a term that
refers to a club whose head is shaped like a driver or fairway wood,
but which is made of metal. It in turn has come to be known as
''Pittsburgh Persimmon,'' a juxtaposition of the Pittsburgh Steel
company and the persimmon wood used in traditional drivers. It's
as much a mongrel as metalwood, but it works. I've also heard
''Hamilton Hardware'' in Canada, because a major steel producer
is located in Hamilton, Ontario. The popularity of the metalwood,
meanwhile, has meant that one must be more specific when describing the club he'll use off the tee. A conventional wood is now a
''wood-wood,'' to distinguish it from the metalwood. And now
there's the ''licorice stick,'' any graphite-shafted club.

Now we're out on the course, where anything can happen. You
can hit a shot that moves sharply from left to right, a slice in common parlance, but also a ''banana ball.'' If you plan to hit the ball
left to right intentionally, then maybe you'll have the courage to
announce it — ''I'm going to fade this, or carve it, or cut it.'' Henry

Longhurst grew up on Bedfordshire, a course west of London that encouraged a fade because the penalty for hitting a hook was severe. This became his modus operandi and led to a common golfing term in England. "Indeed," he wrote in 1958, "I can say with a sort of inverted pride that in certain quite distinguished golfing circles I can claim to have put a new word into the golfing language and that to describe a shot as having a bit of 'Bedfordshire' on it is to be at once understood."

I've hit my share of shots with a bit of Bedfordshire on them, but I also played a course for many years where it was useful to hit the ball right to left on one critical hole in particular. The fourteenth hole at Uplands in Toronto was a long par-four with an out-of-bounds fence immediately to the right and hundreds of yards of open space to the left. It must have been on this hole, coming later in the round, that my hands learned to turn over when coming through the ball, thereby producing all too often a "duck hook," a "quacker," a "shrimp," or a "Corporal Snapper," after a fellow who worked for Scotland Yard. May I then coin a new word for such a shot? I'll call it an "Uplands," as in "You had more Uplands than you needed in that shot, my friend."

Different terrains stimulate new words. You might be playing a course with hard fairways in a wind-swept town in west Texas, as I did at the Ft. Stockton Country Club. I had to keep the ball low and out of the wind; conditions called for "quail-high" shots. Ben Hogan, a native Texan, favored such shots, as does Lee Trevino. They're also called "frozen ropes," because they resemble the line drives that baseball players hit. There's also the "rainbow shot," a pop-up with nothing on it. It's a kite that's out of control in the wind and soon flops to the ground. Or you might have taken too much club, hit the ball well, and "air-mailed" the green.

What of the shot that travels most of its distance along the ground? This "Scottish" shot is also a "bump-and-run" if you've planned it, a "grasshopper" if you haven't. You've "skulled" the shot, hit it "in the forehead," hit a "worm burner." I hit a different kind of shot in an area near St. Andrews, Scotland, called Pittenweem. The shot is called a "Pittenweem pinger," and refers to a shot hit intentionally low and meant to bounce into the green.

Then there's the shot I hit at Tralee in Ireland. Somebody said, "A bit bony, wasn't it?" I knew what he meant. My fingers shivered as the vibrational aftershock of hitting the ball thinly rang up the clubshaft. Another time, while playing at Littlestone on the southeast coast of England, I heard the term "Barnes Wallace," after a player hit the ground before his ball and bounced the clubhead into the ball. The reference is to a type of bomb invented by one Barnes Wallace; the bomb bounces on the ground.

There are so many varieties of miscues. You may have hit a "Billy Graham" or an "Oral Roberts," a shot off the heel of the club, a "healer." Or how about a "chili-dip," where you've hit the ball fat? You've taken a "pork chop" of a divot, as long as a "pizza slice." Maybe you've hit the middle of the ball with the leading edge of your club; you've chopped the ball, which is also known as an "egg." "Chopped egg," your pal says. Or you've hit the top of the ball, "topped" it, or "cold-topped" it. And let's not even talk about the shank. It doesn't need explanation. Golfers refuse to use the word. Instead, they come up with less sinister descriptions, one of my favorites being "Lucy Locket Socket," which I first heard in England, and also "J. Arthur." I was told that there's an English film company called J. Arthur Rank; the slang for the company is "shank," so when a golfer hits such a shot, it's naturally called a "J. Arthur." Do this when you are about to post a good score and you're choking, "gargling peanut butter," that is.

Such shots can result from uneasiness, even for the best players. Maybe the hole is cut on the rear left portion of the sixteenth green at the Augusta National Golf Club, as it is in many final rounds during the Masters. Jack Nicklaus knows that if he misses slightly left, he'll find the pond. But he's in contention and needs a birdie. So he plans to shoot at the pin. But something changes at the top of his swing as his body registers an impulse to protect the shot, and he blocks the ball to the right into a wider area of the green. Nicklaus has "bailed out," taken the safe route.

All kinds of unpleasant things can happen to a golf ball when the player is swinging poorly. He feels like the ball "is coming out of the popcorn popper," as Johnny Miller once told me during a period when he had no idea where the ball would go. It could go anywhere, "up your pant leg or out of the state." Miller was playing "military golf," left, right, left, right, back and forth across the fairway. The golf course is a minefield at such times. On one hole a player hits his ball into the rough, the "cabbage," the "jungle," or "tiger country." He's behind a tree, "in jail." The player who does this too often is losing shots. He's "leaking oil." Soon he'll have to pick up and put the ball away until the next hole. He's "in his pocket," soon to be known as "Dr. Pocket," at least for one hole. If he's driving a cart, he's "bipsic" (ball in pocket, scorecard in cart).

Thank the golfing gods for sand traps, then. They might prevent our errant shots from traveling further into deeper trouble. Hit a trap, the "kitty litter," that is, or the "cat box," or the "desert," and at least you've got a shot. Then again, your ball may have landed in its own mark in the trap and scooped out an area the general shape of a dish, the ball occupying the middle. You've got a "fried egg" to play, or as British Broadcasting Television's Peter Alliss once said, "A bit of poached-eggy there." Still, the golfer has a chance with a "fried egg." He's better off than if his ball had dug deep into the trap to the extent he could hardly see the top of it. That's a "buried" lie. Spare me from those, please, especially when I have little or no green to work with. The ball runs on and on from a buried lie.

Nobody likes to play this kind of golf because it leads to high scores. Even Greg Norman has shot the odd sunset strip. Ninety-nine looks good for the golfer trying to break 100, but it also became known as a "Gretzky," particularly in Canada, where Wayne Gretzky (whose sweater number is ninety-nine) is a national hero because of his brilliance in hockey. Gretzkys are the order of the day when a player has too many "boxcars" on his scorecard — two sixes in a row.

But the nature of golf sometimes prevents such high numbers. The ebb and flow of the game means that you can also get away with plenty on the course. A sharp iron may redeem an errant drive. Good putting might cancel previous errors; in the same way, though, poor putting can ruin the golfer who hits green after green in regulation. That's why it's said that we drive for show and we putt for dough. Golfers know the frustrations of putting and have come up with no end of expressions to cover the subject. First, of course, the player has to reach the green, the dance floor. I've hit shots seventy feet from the hole when I would have been happier fifteen feet away from the pin in the fringe. Maybe I could have chipped in from there, that is, "made a ferret"; a ferret is a burrowing animal that likes to disappear down holes. Some British golfers play for a bit, or unit of money, for each ferret registered. A "golden ferret" occurs when the golfer holes out from a sand trap. That's worth two bits. The green, though, is golf's Holy Grail. "You're dancing," friends tell me, and I shrug my shoulders. Who, after all, wants a seventy-foot putt? That's a lot of "real estate to negotiate," as the television announcers tell us.

But putting is amusing. Consider the putt that rolls toward the center of the hole, but then catches the front lip and rolls all around before returning to its resting place in front of the hole. That's a "three-sixty," given that the putt traveled the full 360-degree circumference of the hole. The expression has its minor variants — the 180 and 270, putts that occur all too frequently, I might add. The golfer who tells his pal that he had a six-footer for birdie at the last but that the ball did a 360 doesn't have to say anything else. He might also say that he has just hit a marguerita, in that the ball went all the way around the lip of the hole without falling in. The reference is to the drink of the same name, in which we place salt around the lip of the glass. Call the putt a 360 or a marguerita. Or say it "burnt the edges." These terms are more effective than saying the ball went all the way around the hole. "You gave it a smell anyway," an Irish companion told me when my putt did a 360 at Lahinch. Nonetheless, a ball sometimes does go in on its way around the hole. If it fell in the opposite side of the hole, it went "in the back door." The putt that falls in after circling the hole completed a "victory lap."

Phrases that describe the flight of the ball or its mode of travel are common. There's the "snake," a putt that twists and turns and wriggles its way across the contours of the green before falling into the hole. Jack Nicklaus holed a forty-five-foot snake for a birdie two on the sixteenth green during the final round of the 1975 Masters and went on to win. He leaped after the putt fell, his club held high. This was an appropriate response to holing a snake at such a time. Snakes are rare, but the term is exact. Every golfer has hit a long putt at one time or another and stood transfixed as it meandered across the green's undulations toward the hole. It's eerie, particularly because we often sense that the ball will go in well before it's even gotten close to the hole. Some golfers put it this way: "The putt was so long that it had to go through four time zones." Another golfer might face a putt that is so long and must travel such a convoluted route that he will say, "I need a transfer to get there from here."

Not every long putt that is holed travels so lurching and winding a road. Sometimes a golfer will take the break out of a putt by hitting it so hard — usually accidentally — that it appears the ball will go far beyond the hole. Suddenly, however, it seems that the ball might have a chance. It's going straight for the hole. "Catch the lip," the player might say, or "Catch a corner." If he's lucky, the ball will zoom toward the front of the hole, catch that lip, and then jump in the air, finally coming back down to drop right in the hole. The hole got in the way and the ball fell. "Slam-dunk," the golfer says, invoking a reference to the basketball shot. The golfer's opponent may respond, "You oughta be called for traveling," since the ball was moving so quickly that it was sure to go well beyond the hole had it not fallen in. The slam-dunk's opposite number is the putt that drops into the hole on its last roll. It "fell in drunk."

But most putts don't fall in. Put it this way: Eighteen putts a round do go in, but they're usually the short ones left after we've worked our way near the hole. How often do we really make putts longer than a couple of feet? Not often enough, that's for sure. A vocabulary of missed putts has arisen to cover the ground.

I remember hitting a ten-foot putt that never looked like it was going to go in. I'd hit the ball tentatively, as if I didn't want it to reach the hole. My partner called this a "qualifying putt" and explained that he had first heard the term from a professional in North Carolina. A golfer who has two putts to survive the thirty-six-hole cut and reach the last two rounds of a tournament doesn't have to try to make a ten-foot putt. Why be aggressive? He can afford to get his first putt close to the hole to ensure that he will qualify. Hence the term "qualifying putt."

But sometimes the tentatively hit putt comes up too short. The golfer is left with a putt of a few feet, no "gimme," as in "I'll give you that one," or, "That's a gimme." Afraid not. The player "should get his tool kit out." He's got some work left. I've also been told to "clean it up," that is, to tap in what's left. The three letters no golfer likes to hear are "U.S.A." — "You're still away." I also like the phrase "There's still a little chicken on the bone yet." Chicken on the bone, indeed; the first time I heard these words, I had to force myself to concentrate on my next putt rather than think about the image the phrase had evoked. Leave too much chicken on the bone too many times and you're liable to be taking a long time on the course, committing the sin of slow play. It's a good idea then to speed things up on the fairways. Play "ready golf." That is, the golfer who is ready, not necessarily the one who is away, plays first.

I, like all golfers, have missed far too many short putts. Sometimes it seems I'm "stickhandling" my way around the greens, back and forth, using my putter as a hockey stick and getting nowhere fast. "Another three-jack," somebody might say after I've three-putted; or I'll be informed that I've just hit into a "triple-play." Crude individuals call the prolonged experience a "three-whack." I don't know where the poor putting comes from, but I do know the name for the problem when it spreads. Did I say "problem"? Amend that to "disease," as in the "yips." Scottish pro Tommy Armour coined the term, and everybody knows what it means. One's hands flit about; wrists break, fingers twitch, the putter blade jumps, anxiety takes over. I'd rather not talk about it. As Henry Longhurst wrote about the yips, "Once you've had 'em, you've got 'em." The yips are also known by their parallel condition, "whiskey fingers." The term is self-explanatory. Oddly, the Scottish drink kummel is also known as "putter's mixture." The cure is the same as the disease.

Putting is unnerving, and the language that has developed around the short strokes conforms to the rule that the more confusing something is, the more effort we will make in trying to understand

and describe it. Did you miss that putt because you couldn't figure the speed of the green? Don't worry. It's not your fault. "Too much ice," somebody said after knocking a putt five feet by the hole. "Grab a chair," a kind-hearted companion might say as the putt zips by the hole, or "Hit a bus," or simply and directly, "Sit down." And what if the green is too slow? That's also not your fault. "This green is as slow as molasses," or "It's like putting in quicksand," or "It's about time they shaved this, don't you think?" Then again, the speed of the green might not be the problem. Maybe the green has too many contours. The ninth green at the Jasper National Park course in Alberta is called "Cleopatra," because designer Stanley Thompson shaped it to remind the golfer from the tee of the lady's contours. Sir Harry Thornton, then head of the Canadian National Railway, couldn't help but notice the view when he played the course with Thompson. He was not pleased.

"Mr. Thompson," he said, "we have been friends for many years. I never thought you would have the audacity to do this to the Canadian National." Thompson was disappointed at Sir Harry's reaction, but he did smooth out some of the undulations. The hole is still called Cleopatra, and it's "tougher to figure than Chinese arithmetic," "harder to read than a Russian novel." Besides, I wonder how Sir Harry Thornton would have felt had he faced the topsy-turvy, roller-coaster greens that are often found in modern courses? "I had me a Dolly Parton putt there," the golfer says, "up and down and over the humps." There's only one way to handle such a green. Watch your playing companions and "go to school" on their putts. Then maybe you'll roll the ball well. It will "turn over" as all successful putts do.

If there's good news on the greens, there's also sharp play on the course. There's the "come-back-tomorrow" shot that usually occurs on a later hole when all is lost and we've given up hope of scoring well. We relax and hit a beautiful shot. The game seems simple. And so, just when we had decided we'd give up the game for a while, we alter our plans to come back tomorrow.

I don't mean to imply that these shots are rare in the course of a round. Not at all. Amateur golfers enjoy watching as a well-struck ball lands on the green and spins back, with "juice." I was watching a pro tournament in Florida when a golfer hit the ball as well as he could, and he knew it. "Chow-chow-chow!" he exclaimed, with obvious enthusiasm. But it took a minute to come up with the chain of associations required to understand what he meant. "Chow-chow-chow" is said after a player has hit a pure shot; it derives from Purina Cat Food, or chow, another word for food. It made sense; had the golfer been able to keep up that standard of play he would have "shot the lights out." He would have shot "nothing," as golfers like to say after they've played what they consider a near-perfect round. It's a day when they're making birdies, that is, "catching some feathers," a day when they might have hit good shots with the one-iron, the "butter knife," or just the "knife," the club many golfers consider the most difficult to hit. Professional golfers especially enjoy such a day when it occurs during the third round of a seventy-two-hole tournament; that's the time to make a move on the field. Saturdays are "moving days." Play poorly that day and it's "Atlas Van Lines." The player has shot himself out of the tournament. It's time to move on.

I've enjoyed studying the language of golf as well as listening to it. The terms "par" and "skins" in particular interest me, and so I have examined their etymology. It's another dimension of the game. Besides, I was bewildered by their usage.

"Par" first. It's a confusing term when viewed from the perspective of how we use the word in everyday language. "How are you feeling?" somebody asks me. "I'm not up to par," I might say, or "I'm a little under par." That is, I'm not feeling well. I'm doing poorly. But when I'm "under par" on the course, I'm doing well. Why does the discrepancy exist? Is it a discrepancy?

The origins of "par" itself aren't clear. It refers to the score that a first-rate golfer would achieve on a hole; it's something to shoot for. It also colors the very way in which we think about the game. A 450-yard par-four might more reasonably be considered a par-five when it's playing into a thirty-mile-an-hour wind, and many golfers would play it more conservatively if it were. Most of us, however, play a hole according to the card rather than what the conditions suggest.

"Par" is no simple matter. Its usage predates "bogey," a term we now think of as referring to one-over par on a hole. Peter Davies is a lexicographer who worked as the editor in chief of the *American Heritage Dictionary* and who wrote the book *Davies' Dictionary of Golfing Terms*. He wrote that the term "bogey" was brought to golf in 1890-1891 by Major Charles Wellman while playing at Great Yarmouth in Norfolk, England.

The major, Davies wrote, "is said to have exclaimed that the standard score of the course was a 'regular Bogey Man,' referring to the then-current music-hall song, 'Hush, hush, hush, here comes the Bogey Man . . . he'll catch you if he can.'" Wellman meant that a good amateur might shoot bogey for the course, but that a lesser player would have difficulty doing so. Davies pointed out that some English courses had in the 1880s assigned a target score to each hole that an amateur could attain. But that standard wasn't easily achieved. Wellman decided that bogey was more reasonable, and soon Dr. Thomas Browne, secretary of Great Yarmouth, took on the term to mean the score a top-class player could achieve. It soon came to mean a total score for eighteen holes of around eighty.

But how did the current meaning of bogey come about? This is unclear, but it does seem that first it was the other way round. Par, as mentioned, was a standard before bogey, according to Davies. It was a stricter interpretation of what constituted expert golf and eventually came to be seen as *the* standard. Some holes actually had the same par and bogey. This is understandable, given that a course with par of seventy-two and bogey of eighty differ by only eight shots. As there are eighteen holes on a course, it is obvious that some holes would be assigned the same par and bogey values.

The value of this is clear, and it might have been helpful to golfers' egos if the meanings had remained. After all, not many golfers can shoot par. A score of eighty is more within reach and allows for a margin of error. I might enjoy running a couple of miles a day, but I don't measure my speed against the fastest runners. I'm content to run at my own pace and gradually improve. That is, I have my own idea of what is right for me, of what is attainable. Hence the term "personal best" in a sport such as running. Bogey, if I can stretch the comparison, is more meaningful and realistic.

Eventually, however, par became the standard by which we measure ourselves as golfers. A bogey came to mean a score of one-over-par, although some British courses still retain the distinction on their scorecards, and even modern dictionaries are unclear as to the word's meaning. The *Pocket Oxford Dictionary* (1986) defines bogey as "par or one more than par on a hole in golf." What's a golfer to do when the authorities on the language can't make up their minds?

But never mind. The original meaning of bogey as the standard a decent amateur might attain has all but disappeared from golf. That form is archaic. And as much as bogey in its current meaning of one-over-par might be a significant accomplishment for many golfers, they still think of par as the real achievement. Bogey was once benign; now it's not such a friend. The *Pocket Oxford Dictionary* makes the point, defining "bogy" (no "e") as "an evil spirit, devil, goblin; awkward thing or circumstance." "Bogy" or "bogey," I agree; it's evil indeed, and often awkward, especially when it comes in a better-ball competition when one's partner is out of the hole. I've also heard the term used outside golf, as in "I bogeyed that job," after a person, for instance, makes a mess of wallpapering a room.

But what about the divergent meanings of "under par"? The meaning of the term in golf seems the only obvious example of the phrase being used positively. Even in sports where a lower number or score is valued, as in running a mile in three minutes fifty-two seconds rather than three fifty-five, the runner doesn't say he ran lower, but faster. The only meaningful way to compare performance in golf is to say one player shot lower than another.

The phrase "under par" is an example of what linguists refer to as language-crossing groups. The golfer on the course means something different from somebody off the course, where the situational demands change. Jargon distinguishes language communities. Take a phrase out of its milieu and the term can have a different meaning. The aforementioned golf term "bailed out" is another illustration of the point. It connotes a conservative and intelligent action outside golf, one taken out of prudence. The same meaning might apply on the course when a golfer plans to take a conservative, safe route. But it suggests fear if the golfer bails out unintentionally. This happens all the time; we aim over the trap right at the hole, but then hit the ball well away from the bunker. And we know we played a defensive shot.

As for me, I'm trying to ignore the meanings of par, bogey, under par, and above par. If I'm tired, then par might be eighty-five. If I'm feeling terrific, then maybe it's seventy-three. That's par for me, or bogey, or my target score, or my standard score. It's hard to say.

If golf is a few centuries old, then so are its participants' propensities for wagering on the result. One of the most popular forms of wagering is known as "skins." I've played this game for years, always for the sheer sport, of course. A player wins a skin when he scores lower on a hole than any of his companions. Should I make a four while the other players in my group score higher, then I win a skin. No skin is won if two or more players tie for low score on the hole; it's two tie, all tie. A skin is worth a set amount, usually a dollar in my case, and sometimes we play double for birdies. We might also play "carryovers," in which the bet from a tied hole is carried over to the next hole.

Skins games have become popular with professionals, or at least with the promoters who organize golf events. Jack Nicklaus, Curtis Strange, Lee Trevino, Arnold Palmer, Fuzzy Zoeller, and Seve Ballesteros have all participated in the games, and always for large sums of money that the sponsors provide. Trevino made a hole in one that was worth $175,000 at one such event. But these skins games aren't genuine, because the golfers aren't playing for their own money. Amateurs who play for a dollar of their own cash might well feel more pressure than the professionals do while playing for large sums that sponsors are putting up. We amateurs know the true meaning of skins. The requirement is simple: Play well or you get skinned. The game is also called "cleaners," as in, "I took you to the cleaners" or "I got cleaned out."

As the skins games became widespread in the professional ranks, I became interested in the origins of the term. *A Dictionary of American English* provided the first clue. It defines skin as follows:

To beat, to eclipse, to beat a person "all hollow" in a game; a fraudulent game, a swindle. Next came the *Desk Book of Idioms and Idiomatic Phrases*, which defines "skin game" as a confidence game, a swindle, a trick, especially at cards. The *New Dictionary of American Slang* defines skin as a dollar bill; to trounce, to victimize, cheat, swindle.

I wasn't getting anywhere. Each of these definitions suggested something underhanded about a skin, or about skinning somebody. Oddly, then, the most telling definition comes from the *Dictionary of the Underworld*. To skin, the dictionary points out, is to strip a man of all his money at play. Now this is more like it. Golfers feel this as they stand over a putt that could win a skin. There's a sense of emptying your opponents' pockets by filling your own; you also know that if wishes and hexes had power you'd never make the putt, given the crossed fingers of the other golfers in the group. To skin, then, means to extract money. At least it means that while we're at play.

But what of the word "skin" as a noun? William Safire, a writer on language for *The New York Times*, has said that the term "skin" for a dollar probably derived from the early pioneer practice of using animal skins as a form of currency. Professional golfer Doug Sanders, no stranger to gambling on the golf course, thinks it may have been a term used around caddie shacks in the early part of this century to refer to a money game.

"Dollar skins, guys?" The phrase means more to me now when I hear it asked on the first tee. I'm connected to pioneers and to con artists. Words are links. I'm sure I didn't realize while playing my first course that the links were so extensive and that the game could be a passageway to the language.

And what of "links"? This is a golf word for the ages, bound up with the ancient history of the game, a far more interesting word than "course," but one whose meaning is easily obscured. What do we mean, anyway, when we refer to a links course? That double word is in truth not even a legitimate phrase, for links stands alone. It takes into account the idea of a golf course, but refers also to the land upon which golf was first played in Scotland and which today still offers ideal turf and terrain for the game.

The Old Course in St. Andrews is a links because, as Robert Price points out, the land beside the sea is a result of what he terms "accumulations of blown sand." All links are seaside courses, the consequences of rises and falls in sea levels over a period of tens of thousands of years. Price explains that the sea last retreated 6,500 years ago, when it exposed beaches up to a mile wide. The wind acted upon the sand to create dunes systems, while also creating the ridges, hummocks, and mounds so characteristic of such links as the Old Course, Royal Dornoch in the north of Scotland, and Machrihanish in the west. Similar movements took place all along the English, Irish, and Welsh coastlines, so that a portion of the United Kingdom's coastlines is now linksland. Dunes grasses grow, as do heather and gorse. Hence the untamed look of the golfing linksland, although Price makes the point that man has occupied the links for more than 5,000 years and has surely influenced the land's development.

Still, a links is as close as we can get to the game as it was played centuries ago. The courses themselves, then, provide links to golf's early days. I rarely play the Old Course without picturing Old Tom Morris, the four-time British Open champion whose last win was in 1867 and who was also the head greenkeeper at the links. To walk across the Swilcan Burn bridge onto the first green at the Old Course is to feel a link with Old Tom. The "auld grey toon by the sea" brings me back to the game's roots.

Peter Davies shows that the word "links" derives from Old Scottish "lynkis," meaning "ridges, hummocks," and also from the Old English "hlincas," meaning "rough, open ground," the plural of "hlinc" — "ridge, bank, hummocky ground." He also points out that the word is unrelated to "link" as in a "bond, piece of chain."

Lexicographically speaking, Davies is correct. "Links" *is* unrelated to "link." But I prefer to think otherwise. The effective swing is a linked sequence of movements. A golf course is a linked series of holes, as any skilled golf course architect knows. The routing of the holes is as important as the holes themselves. Meanwhile, I'm linked to early golf whenever I play the game; all it takes to get me back is a three-quarter shot into the wind toward a green shrouded in mist.

Golf's entertaining vocabulary adds to the game. The jargon of golf is another way of enjoying the game. It's any golfer's choice. You can drive the ball long and down the middle of the fairway or you can rip it down the pike. You can hit a good iron into the green or you can smooth it in there. You can roll the ball into the center of the hole or you can pop it into the heart. I'll take the latter every time because it's another link in the game. Golf isn't school, but it can be a means of learning another language.

# NINE

# Links Between Friends

The name Rex Revere is not well known in golfing circles. Even the closest friends and colleagues of this thirteen-handicap golfer born in Binghamton, New York, may not be aware of him. There's a good reason for this. Rex Revere is a pseudonym for a Toronto educator. He took on his new identity after he and a friend were making such a hash of one round that they decided they should be playing under assumed names. Rex Revere was ideal, as it is obviously a phony name but might at the same time be construed as a glamorous stage name. Rex, like many golfers I have met and with whom I have become friends, believes that golf is a world apart from the planet he inhabits on a daily basis. The results he achieves on the course are often not those he would want reported to the world at large, and so he has chosen a stage name to preserve his anonymity. It is one way for him to acknowledge that he drops his professional identity on the course, where he becomes a golfer.

Rex is one of my closest friends. We would never have become

such pals without golf. The game has been a way for us to spend
time together. We have traveled to various courses and tournaments,
and we have always looked forward to the next visit, the next game.
How often, after all, does one spend four solid hours with somebody
these busy days?

A golf course provides a nearly Utopian environment in which
friendships can flourish. Rex and I always walk when we play, so
that we have a chance to catch up on each other's news. Conversation comes easily as we walk down a fairway; we move to our own
shots, then intersect again as we make our way toward the green.
As the game alternates between performance and contemplation,
so does our interaction shift between conversation and shared
silence. Sometimes the rounds that bring people closest are those
in which they say the least: a few holes played late on a summer
evening when the course is quiet and the air cooled; a hike through
the leaves on a sparkling autumn day when the trees are showing
their colors. Once, in the fall, Rex and I were partners in a foursomes, or alternate-shot, match. I let him down on far too many
occasions, but when next we spoke he apologized for having hit
a poor drive on the seventeenth hole when we were two down. It's
just like a friend in golf to do that: He'll tell you it was his fault,
and he'll believe it. Golfers identify with each other, and this is a
strong foundation for friendship. The drive on the seventeenth was
really the only bad shot Rex hit all day.

My friendship with Rex started twenty years ago, shortly after
he moved to Toronto. Later he started what he calls the Tour de
Farce. The Tour has now grown to a dozen events, with about a
half-dozen full-time participants. Rex has written in the annual Tour
de Farce media guide about member Bob Fourapples, who plays
out of the Kemosabi Golf and Country Club, that he "is often seen
carrying on metaphysical discussions with ornamental shrubbery,
and insists on sucking on a mouthful of pebbles during the heat
of tournament competition in order, as he puts it, 'to restore the
mineral balance in my body.'" Then there's Zen Cohen, a recent
addition to the Tour who, despite his unorthodox swing, "continues
his relentless Siddharthan search for the rhythm, although to date,

the closest he has come to that elusive state of bliss seems to be a sort of amphetamine tango.''

We, the members of the Tour de Farce — Tourists, as we call ourselves — gather regularly in friendship to play such tournaments as the Winter Rules Open, the season-opener played as soon as courses use regular greens, and often contested in mud and cold. There's the Dog Day Afternoon, which must be played in terrible conditions in November, that is, driving rain and cold, preferably sleet. There's also the UFOpen and the Par Excellence, where we are joined by such guests as Seve de la Stance-Formie, Noah Vail, and Allen Adaze-Work. The Garbage Bag Open is the Tour de Farce's version of the Masters; it's our rite of spring, after which we present a green garbage bag cut to fit the winner, much as the Augusta National Golf Club presents its green club jacket to the Masters champion immediately after play has ended. My greatest triumph has been in the Golden Bear, where I defeated both Zen Cohen and Rex Revere by a narrow margin; my reward was the wooden head of a Golden Bear driver, so named in honor of Jack Nicklaus, the Golden Bear himself. I have given the clubhead a prominent place in my home, while the Tour de Farce has an important place in my heart. I might add that Rex Revere is a sensible gentleman. His wife and daughter consider him a most responsible fellow.

The encounters and friendships that golf offers are an important part of why we play the game. It's a way to another person, alternating companionship and solitude while opening us up to each other. I have been fortunate to make friends all over the golfing world, and I am sure that this is the case for nearly everybody who plays the game regularly. Years ago I visited the Royal Dornoch Golf Club far in the north of Scotland; I planned to stay only a day or two but stayed ten, having met Lesley Marsh, a talented golfer from Newcastle-upon-Tyne, England, who has represented her county in tournaments. Day after day, we hit balls together on an old airport landing field near the course, then played a few holes together in the twilight. We have met again in the years since at such courses as Gullane, east of Edinburgh, and at the Lookout Point Golf Club in Fonthill, Ontario, the only course that Australian Walter Travis designed in Canada.

I also remember the time I sat with C. Ross (Sandy) Somerville in his hometown of London, Ontario. Sandy won six Canadian Amateurs from 1926 to 1937, and in 1932 won the United States Amateur. He played the 1934 Masters, when he made the first hole in one at the Augusta National Golf Club. He got another at the London Hunt Club in 1980, the year I met him. Sandy was then seventy-seven, and as we sat in his home he related stories that took me back to another time.

Somerville summed up the evolution of the golf swing in as neat a fashion as I have ever heard. "A sweep, a swing, and a hit," is the way he explained the three eras. Old Tom Morris used the long hickory shafts when he won his four British Opens in the last third of the nineteenth century. Bobby Jones was a swinger as clubs changed to a more modern configuration, while Ben Hogan, Arnold Palmer, and Jack Nicklaus hit the ball with the modern, strong steel shafts.

I learned things from Somerville, as I always do from somebody who has been around golf for a long time. He told me that he switched to a lighter driver when he felt himself tiring toward the end of a long match or tournament. Sometimes he changed from a driver to the lighter two-wood toward the end of a round. I asked him the basic principle of golf. "Hit the ball," he said.

I also learned from James Coe, an eighty-one-year-old gentleman who was no longer able to golf due to a stroke. He was born in Yorkshire, England, caddied three rounds a day as a ten year old, and also learned the game while playing a four-hole course he and his friends contrived at the edge of his village. "The holes were coffee tins," he told me in his home in the country north of Toronto. "We made a little green with a mower, about as big as this room. Just banging the ball around, having a lot of fun, having a go at it." Coe soon hit the ball around the hills and the fields and the moors, and then he watched the six-time British Open champion Harry Vardon in 1920 and Bobby Jones in his Grand Slam year of 1930. "Vardon had a lovely swing," Coe recalled. "He had colossal hands.

They say that when he went to dinner he didn't like to put his hands on the table.''

James Coe kept talking and I kept listening. He came to Canada in 1934, joined the Summit club north of Toronto in 1937, and remembers dressing in top hats and tails for dinners and dances, the spring hyacinths and daffodils, nights on the verandas overlooking the eighteenth fairway and green, singing in the showers and barbershop quartets at the club.

These meetings are as much a part of golf as the well-played shot. "Life gives you bounces," Coe told me as he sat in his chair, a blanket over his knees. "It's a devil what does go on. I always say enjoy life to the full while you can." He was looking at a framed photograph of Abbeydale, his home course in England, as he spoke.

I wish Coe could have met Jack Sandy, a golfer who was ninety-four when I joined him for some golf at the Oakdale Golf and Country Club in Toronto. We met at 7:30 one morning for a few holes, Sandy's daily course of action. He took only his putter and an orange ball, put the ball on a tee, and hit it solidly. The ball flew at ankle height before rolling to a stop sixty yards away. This was the beginning of an outing that Sandy said he could not do without. We played ten holes in less than two hours. I was walking with a man who had climbed mountains in the Swiss Alps, who had played baseball and boxed and eventually golfed. He used to carry only a three-wood, five-iron, seven-iron, and nine-iron. "I could never hit the ball very far," he said, "so I made a study of approaching and putting." His eyesight deteriorated by the time he was ninety, which is when he began to use a putter exclusively. He was able to tell where the ball was going by the feel of his swing and the way the ball sounded off the face of the club.

"I never think about the score," Sandy mentioned as we strolled. "I'm out for the walk, the enjoyment of the game. I like the natural life. I like to stop on the benches and listen to the birds. That's beautiful music. I think we're very lucky to be able to do so on the course, where it's so healthy."

Sandy had some advice for score-obsessed golfers. "If a person is irritated because he's scoring poorly, I think he should give up golf. But I've found that the little white pill takes away your problems. Sometimes, when I get up at 4:30, I say, 'Well, should I or shouldn't I go out to the course?' But I always come out. You know my parents used to have a saying in Yiddish. It meant, 'Where do we get the days of old?' That's a beautiful phrase. I think they wanted to know how they could be young again.''

Jack Sandy was young again on the course. His back was straight as he addressed the ball. He took the club back smoothly and simply, and then imparted a clean hit to the ball. He showed me that the swing didn't have to be complicated. I could learn about the swing from watching his form. Professionals weren't the only people who knew the game.

When thinking of people I have met through golf, I reflect on my friendship with Canadian writer Trent Frayne. As much as the Masters is an annual rite of spring, our nearly annual rite is to walk Augusta National Golf Club's eighteen holes at least once during tournament week. We do so early one morning well before the golfers start. There's nobody around, and the course is ours. Our first walk together at Augusta led to a friendship I treasure. We have never played a round of golf together, but walking a course without playing produces its own quiet pleasures.

But sometimes the game offers us more than friendship. It can become a way for two people to learn about each other and form a relationship that becomes a focal point of their lives. The first person I got to know via golf was my father, Percy Rubenstein. Much later I became friends with George Knudson, Canada's finest professional golfer. In the way of the world, I delivered the eulogy at Knudson's funeral in Toronto on January 27, 1989. My father, who held Knudson in high regard and who had followed him for years — they were both born in Winnipeg, Manitoba — also attended his funeral. My dad died less than four months later, and then I began to write this book, all the while aware of how inextricably bound up with golf, and each other, we all were. The game gave me room and time to know my father, and for him to know me, and then it introduced me to Knudson.

I've been struck by how often fathers and sons reach each other through golf. I don't know what it is, maybe the time that the game makes available, maybe the easy freedom of being outdoors with a purpose in mind, perhaps the ways in which a child can express himself while still under the caring eyes of his father.

I was a kid when I got to know my dad through golf. He introduced me to the game in a variety of ways as we played together and visited golf tournaments together. One of my strongest memories is of watching Gene Littler win the 1965 Canadian Open over Jack Nicklaus at the Mississauga Golf and Country Club near Toronto. I was a teen-ager by then, immersed in the game. My dad and I followed Littler and Nicklaus the last nine holes. I noticed not only Littler's golf, but how often he looked over to his own young son, and how keen the boy was to see how his father was doing.

Years later, I watched Curtis Strange win the 1988 United States Open at The Country Club in Brookline, Massachusetts. Strange was already one of golf's best players, but he hadn't yet won a major championship. He was waiting to win one so that he could publicly thank his father, who had died when Strange was fourteen, for supporting his golf. Strange had won Jack Nicklaus's Memorial Tournament in Dublin, Ohio, just a few weeks prior to the United States Open and had thought that he might thank his dad there, at a tournament that is as close to being a major as there is without being one. But he decided to wait because he felt he'd yet win a major. Strange was a strong-minded golfer, and he had what he called a "fire in my belly." He was also honest and direct, qualities I'd seen while watching and chatting with him. There was something about him, some line of force directing him. I wondered if he was motivated in part by the memory of his father, Thomas Wright Strange, and what he had given him.

Strange did his father proud at Brookline. He got into an eighteen-hole play-off with English virtuoso Nick Faldo after being required to get up and down from a greenside bunker on the last hole of regulation play. He won the play-off 71-75, and then he — cool, willful Curtis Strange — showed his emotions. He sat down in the interview area at Brookline and showed us how he and his father and golf were intimately connected. It was the day after Father's Day.

"I have to thank my dad," Strange said, his voice breaking. "This is for my dad. That's all I can say."

Later Strange spoke again about his father, a golf professional who was good enough to play in the 1963 United States Open. He introduced his son to golf when he was nine years old and taught him the fundamentals. "They're still with me," Strange said. "He taught me things I still think about every day. I just wish he could have been here. This means what every little boy dreams about when he plays late in the afternoon with three or four balls and pretends he's Snead, Hogan, Nicklaus, and Strange. It means all the time and effort paid off."

Strange was asked if he had thought of his dad during the play-off round.

"Only once or twice did my mind wander to my dad," he answered. "Last year (during the 1987 United States Open at the Olympic Club in San Francisco), a good friend of mine told me on the tenth tee to win it for my dad. It was Father's Day. I went to the tee with tears in my eyes. I didn't want that to happen today."

That didn't happen. But something else did. Strange won the United States Open, and then the feelings of a champion golfer for his father burst through. He had carried the memory of himself and his dad on the golf course for twenty years. The golf course brought them together in important ways as father and son, teacher and student.

My father's Spalding Top-Flite clubs are in a golf bag next to me. A dozen or so golf balls are in the pocket, and for all I know he may have used them the last time we played together. That was in the spring of 1987 on a golf course not far from the home where we first played the game together. He had some heart problems, but still he walked the course. Walking was his favorite part of golf. It gave him time to look around.

Most weekend mornings when I was a kid, we woke up at five o'clock to ensure we'd get a tee time by seven at a nearby public course. His friend Willie accompanied us as we played the rough-and-tumble layout. My dad was a left-handed golfer who wrote right-handed; he was also a left-handed quarterback with the Air

Force Bombers, as they were known; the team was the forerunner of the Winnipeg Blue Bombers in the Canadian Football League. I was a right-handed golfer who writes left-handed. Willie? He provided us with laughs for years when we recollected an incident at the par-three fifteenth hole at Don Valley, our favorite public course. The hole wasn't more than 120 yards and was made even shorter because it played from an elevated tee. Willie decided to use a four-wood, which I thought was about nine clubs too many. "What are you doing?" I asked. "I'll just pop it up in the air with a small swing," Willie answered, as if to say, "What do you think I'm doing?" The ball popped up just as he said it would and landed right in the middle of the green. That was my introduction to shot-making. My dad and I chuckled all the way to the clubhouse, wondering why Willie ever decided to hit such a shot.

Those were wonderful days. Golf was in the air around our home. The front room turned into a miniature golf course when I placed plastic cups all around for targets. I also used the legs of chairs and tables. The soft pillows of the sofa were ideal landing spots for chip shots, and the carpet in the corridor served as a putting green. Just outside the front door, meanwhile, was a lawn not more than fifteen yards long that ended in a ditch at the edge of the road. The ditch was wide enough for me and my dad to stand in, and it sloped just enough so that we could place golf balls at various angles and lies and then try to loft them across the street, where a neighbor's tree was the target.

My dad helped me dig a few holes in our back yard; the first hole was 25 yards long or so — about the length of the yard — and began on an elevated tee on top of a hill outside my bedroom, underneath which was a septic tank. This was the beginning of the Joicey Boulevard Golf Club, annual dues twenty-five cents. I was president and secretary and my dad was treasurer. We played the course spring and summer evenings after dinner, my dad on one side facing me as he chipped the ball left-handed, me opposite him chipping the ball right-handed. His swing was rhythmic, and his short back-yard shots taught me that you didn't have to swing hard to make solid contact with the ball. The course was short and our walks to our next shots were just a few yards, but we could say a lot in the space of an evening. After dark, we turned on the lights in the back of the house or played by moonlight. I liked to hit full shots across the neighbors' fences and back yards; first next door, then, stretching out, two and three and four houses down. I broke a few windows in my time and sometimes got into an argument with a neighbor. I liked hitting the ball high, but every so often the ball would hit some hydro wires and wreak havoc with his television. My dad suggested I hit the ball lower, if I could, but when I didn't he acted as a peacemaker with our neighbor.

That was my routine most evenings — playing my back-yard course, chipping and pitching golf balls over the fences. My dad often played along, and when we finished we sat on the hill that represented the first tee and listened to baseball and football games while drinking loganberry juice. On weekend mornings we were up before dawn for our round with Willie. Then we would return home and cut the grass as short as possible to prepare for the next week's play.

My dad also took me to watch the pros whenever they were in the area. I accompanied him on August 16, 1961, to watch Arnold Palmer and Gary Player in an exhibition at the Scarboro Golf and Country Club in the eastern part of Toronto. Two years later we followed big George Bayer during the Canadian Open at Scarboro. Bayer was playing the long, par-five sixth hole when my father told me to have a good look. "Watch him whack it," my dad said. "He could reach the green from here." But Bayer topped the ball 150 yards down the fairway. My dad was surprised, but he understood. Things didn't always go well in golf.

These were sweet times. When we played, we were alone together in a green valley, he pulling his clubs on a cart, me slinging my clubs over my shoulder. The first encounters I remember with my dad were through sports — throwing the football around was a staple, as was knocking about in golf. Maybe these were paradigms for the relationship we continued as I became an adult, as he grew older and his heart grew weaker. We had time together in and around golf. I sensed his pride when I played a series of controlled shots, and also when I took a chance. He'd said something memorable to me when we threw the football around. "If you can touch it, you can catch it," he suggested. I extended the idea to golf, figuring that I might be able to pull off a risky shot if it were just within my range. The par-four tenth hole at the course we played swung left around a river; the safe route was to the right, which left a mid-iron to a green set in a glade. But I liked to turn the ball around the corner when I was feeling good. Most times I felt very good by the time I reached the tenth. The dew on the grass had gone wherever dew goes, the morning sun was higher, and I was warmed up. My dad didn't mind what shot I played, but I think he enjoyed it when I flexed my golfing muscles. He especially liked watching me hit a long, straight drive. "My son's got all the shots," he'd tell people. But he told me first, "If you can touch it, you can catch it."

When winter came, we watched golf together on television, and on weekday evenings and some weekend afternoons he drove me to the Toronto School of Golf, in a nearby plaza. There were a few mats from which we could hit balls into a canvas, a supply of golf magazines, and enough good-natured golf talk to get us through the winter. My dad's coffee became lukewarm as he watched me hit balls. Who knew where they were going? I was hitting into a canvas mat ten feet away, but that didn't matter. My dad waited for the smack of the clubface against the ball. He liked to watch me swing. He hated lukewarm coffee, but he drank it.

The spring of 1966 arrived and, in June, the United States Open. I was eighteen now, and more interested in playing golf than in watching it. Curtis Strange has told me that he used to watch Arnold Palmer and Jack Nicklaus on television when he was thirteen or fourteen, while sitting in the golf shop at the club where he played and his dad worked. "I wouldn't even wait for the finish," Strange said. "I'd go out and play."

I know how Strange felt. Golf is a participant sport. There was honest pleasure in watching it, but a kid's real place was on the course. I was hitting a few shots in the yard when my dad called me into the house. He was excited. "Come on in. This kid Johnny Miller is doing great. He's only nineteen, an amateur." Miller played well that United States Open at the Olympic Club in San Francisco and then went on to his successful career as a professional. My dad wanted me to see him in his finest hour as an amateur.

It wasn't much later that my dad and I drove down to the Foxfire Country Club in Pinehurst, North Carolina, where he'd rented a golf villa for a week. I have a picture of him at Foxfire. He's smoking his favorite cigar while returning a fairway wood to his golf bag. There's a smile on his face, and why not? Golf was being kind to us. Life was being kind to us, a father and a son together in early spring sunshine on a course surrounded by tall pines.

Soon it was the winter of 1968, and we were thinking about our next golf journey together while following from afar George Knudson's play in Arizona. Knudson had already won four PGA Tour events and was much admired for a technically perfect swing. Knudson had studied Ben Hogan's swing when he arrived on the PGA Tour in the late 1950s, and, before long, people were saying he looked more like Hogan than Hogan himself. He knew where the ball was going every time. My father had followed Knudson and, now, here he was, winning in Phoenix and then contending the next week in Tucson. Could he win two in a row? I borrowed my dad's car to drive down to the corner to pick up the morning paper. I opened it in the car to the sports pages. Knudson had won again. I was as excited for him as if he were family. Little did I know that one day we would consider each other as part of the same family, that nearly twenty years later he would ask me to write the book that explained what he knew about the golf swing, and that we would work on it together while he was battling cancer.

Long before all this happened, however, Knudson and I had met, and soon after, he and my dad met. I liked the way things were going. I had cast my fate to the golfing wind, as it were, shifted in that direction years before when my dad had helped me sink tins into the ground for the Joicey Boulevard Golf Club. My dad had a smooth swing, although he never played enough or worked hard enough on his game to achieve the low handicap of which he was capable. His well-timed swing helped me understand that rhythm was important, and his good nature on the course helped me see that I shouldn't take this game for granted, this being out in the

open and with others in the seasons when golfers met, in good lies
and bad, on easy courses and hard.

My dad met Knudson one evening in the late 1970s at my parents'
home. Knudson and I had met at a golf school that taught not the
golf swing but concentration. Knudson had dropped by to visit and
was soon involved in the program. Now we were conducting a small
think tank on the subject, and George was contributing his ideas.
He had left the PGA Tour around the same time in favor of teaching
and went on to become as devoted to communicating his ideas as
he had been to developing a swing that worked better the more
pressure he put on it. We spoke for hours that night in my parents'
home. I remember how stimulating it was, how rapt was my dad's
attention, how interested he was to hear Knudson's views.

I golfed with Knudson from time to time after that, but our most
productive hours were spent around his pool in north Toronto,
overlooking a ravine. It was quiet there. The peace in nature
reminded Knudson of Cypress Point, his favorite golf course. We'd
sit out there and talk about golf, and soon we were talking about
anything and everything. George felt that every person had a gift,
and that the deepest pleasure to be had was in trying to fulfill one's
potential. He encouraged me to write, and the very morning after
I had my first article published in a major magazine he phoned me.
"You've got your foot in the door," he said. "Just keep writing.
Good things will happen."

George believed what he said, and he started to use his knowledge
of the golf swing as a means of reaching people. He taught from
the late 1970s until he contracted lung cancer in June 1987, just
after we had begun work on *The Natural Golf Swing*. "I'm not
just teaching golf," he said. "I'm teaching people how to get the
most out of themselves and how to relax while doing it." He meant
to continue doing so even after he was diagnosed as having cancer.

The cancer went into remission, and George eventually played
in the 1988 Peter Gzowski Invitational at the Briars Golf and Country Club across the road from the southern shore of Lake Simcoe,
fifty miles north of Toronto. Gzowski is the host of "Morningside,"
the popular radio program broadcast daily across Canada. He also
likes golf and had returned in his middle years to the game he played

quite well as a boy. Many mornings he was the first player on the course. His interest in golf and his concern for others had led to his organizing a tournament to raise money that would go toward programs to help reduce illiteracy in Canada. Knudson believed in the cause and wouldn't miss the Invitational if he could help it. Despite feeling weakened, he played his way happily around the Briars' pretty course.

George could be an emotional person. Tears once came to his eyes when he was practicing for a match in São Paulo, Brazil, because the crowd started applauding his warm-up. He simply loved hitting the golf ball as well as he could. Tommy Bolt, a skilled shot-maker himself, played with George during the last round of the 1967 New Orleans Open, which George won. "They can't beat you, son," Bolt told George that day. "You're too good."

Thinking about George now, I remember his zest for life. I walked into his home one evening when the cancer was in remission to find him doing push-ups against the wall. He told me that when he was a kid he used to hit any object on the ground, such as a tin, toward a target. Another evening he showed me a couple of handmade get-well cards that Sandra and Dorothy Haines, two talented young golfers with whom he had worked, had sent him. And he didn't flinch when he was weak — when chemotherapy and radiation were taking their toll. "Golf is good training for a good constitution," he told me. Or, as he also said, "It's not what you achieve that counts, but what you attempt to achieve."

George's feelings for golf didn't depend on his score or on the conditions being ideal. In some ways, George appreciated golf the most when the weather was harsh. One late fall day when he was well, he went out with me and Norm Mogil, my friend who had won the 1962 Canadian Junior. George bundled himself up and then put on a shot-making display. After a while it didn't matter what I was doing, or how Norm was playing. We were content just to watch George play chess with the course, moving the ball around at will.

George could make even non-participants believe that golf was the best game in the world. He was immersed in the act of hitting the ball and being on the course, and while the cancer was in remission he looked forward to playing the Senior PGA Tour. His friends also looked forward to that time; we felt he would do well, but it was more important that he would be able to show that the game could be played with artistry at any age.

Eventually, however, the cancer returned. George tried to remain optimistic though he was in great pain. He retreated into his mind and his mind's eye. He had studied art at high school in Winnipeg, and at one time had to choose between developing that talent or his ability in golf. As a golfer, of course, George kept his artist's eye, and he never lost his vision. One afternoon in the hospital when George was quite ill, he visualized Cypress Point. He spoke softly about the places he had seen as a golfer, the people he had met, and the life he had led while mastering the art and science of hitting a golf ball. Cypress Point was in his mind's eye all the time.

"I played eighteen holes there in my mind this morning," George said. "It was just like I imagined it: the fog heavy, that big lone cypress tree down on the first fairway, the view of the water from the green. My favorite spot."

George said so much that is worth remembering. "You have to give up control to gain control," he advised when telling his students that they could swing properly as long as they started in the right position and then, through transferring weight back and forth, flowed through to their target. The path of the club would take care of itself. His Number One piece of advice went like this: "Never do anything at the expense of balance."

One evening at the hospital he told me what he hoped people might learn from him. "I want people to come alive," he said. "I want them to use their senses."

George died not long after he said these words. Messages of condolence to his wife Shirley and their three sons arrived from many people. Among them were ones from Jack Nicklaus and Johnny Pott, a contemporary of George's on the PGA Tour with whom the previous spring he had played his last event, the Legends of Golf better-ball in Austin, Texas. Shirley asked me to deliver the eulogy at his funeral. The church was packed with members of the Canaian golf community. My father attended. He, too, had become Knudson's friend, and as I looked out over the crowd while I spoke,

I again realized that friendship was not negotiable. It couldn't be invented. It came from common bonds; on this day, we were gathered because of Knudson's death, but it was his life, and golf, that had brought us together.

I went to the Masters in April 1989, nearly three months after George died. Curtis Strange and I spoke about George. The two golfers had the utmost respect for each other. Strange knew what kind of ball-striker George was, and George felt Strange had the best swing in golf. I chatted with Strange about his father, and the aftermath of his win at the 1988 United States Open. On my return from the Masters, I spoke with my dad about our attending our first British Open together at Royal Troon in Scotland come July. But that wasn't to be.

On the night of May 10, I went to a political lecture in Toronto. The speaker talked about the troubled world we live in and left the audience with the message that effort and hope were crucial to our making it a better place. The next day, a column I had written appeared in *The Globe and Mail*. The subject was a tournament that was honoring George and that would raise money for the newly established George Knudson Cancer Research Fund at Princess Margaret Hospital in Toronto. My dad read the column and called me at 5:00 P.M. to talk about it and ask about the lecture I had attended the previous evening. We chatted about the importance of hope. That was our last conversation. He died of a heart attack two hours later.

My dad had a golfer's soul. He was happy no matter where he played or watched the game — basic Tuxedo Golf Course in Winnipeg, fabulous Oakland Hills outside Detroit, or our back-yard course. He always remembered the role golf played in our lives together.

I often drive past the golf course where I first caddied, then turn along Joicey Boulevard as I make my way around Toronto. My boyhood home was torn down long ago for a new house, but I can see the back yard from a street around the corner. The hill above the septic tank that served as the first tee of the Joicey Boulevard Golf Club is gone, but the yard is otherwise unchanged. I stop my car and I picture my dad and me chipping balls around the old course. Then I think of us at any one of numerous golf courses, hitting the ball, chasing it, and hitting it again. I repeated the ritual years later with George Knudson, when we spent hours together on a practice field. I was happy to sit on the end of a golf bag and watch the maestro hit balls.

The 1989 Peter Gzowski Invitational was held within a month of my father's death. I was unable to attend and missed an important part of the day when Peter, another friend in golf and because of golf, spoke about an award that would commemorate George's feeling for golf. The first annual George Knudson silver tee was awarded to the person who had the most pleasure during the round. George's wife Shirley presented the pin to Danielle Nadon, a talented golf professional in Quebec.

My dad and George showed me that the best reasons to play golf are for the humble pleasures and the sense of well-being it bestows upon us. I was ready to go out on the course again a couple of months after my father died. I called Rex Revere. We put the clubs over our shoulders and made our way down the course, heading out for another game.